# GLOUCESTERSHIRE HERO

# GLOUCESTERSHIRE HERO

*Brigadier Patsy Pagan's*
*Great War Experiences*

*by*
Peter Rostron

Pen & Sword
**MILITARY**

First published in 2015 by
Pen and Sword Military

*An imprint of*
Pen & Sword Books Ltd
47 Church Street
Barnsley
South Yorkshire
S70 2AS

ISBN 9781473843745

Printed and bound in England
By CPI Group (UK) Ltd, Croydon, CR0 4YY

Pen & Sword Books Ltd incorporates the Imprints of Pen & Sword
Aviation, Pen & Sword Family History, Pen & Sword Maritime, Pen
& Sword Military, Pen & Sword Discovery, Pen & Sword Politics, Pen
& Sword Atlas, Pen & Sword Archaeology, Wharncliffe Local History,
Wharncliffe True Crime, Wharncliffe Transport, Pen & Sword Select, Pen
& Sword Military Classics, Leo Cooper, The Praetorian Press, Claymore
Press, Remember When, Seaforth Publishing and Frontline Publishing

*For a complete list of Pen & Sword titles please contact*
**PEN & SWORD BOOKS LIMITED**
47 Church Street, Barnsley, South Yorkshire, S70 2AS, England
E-mail: enquiries@pen-and-sword.co.uk
Website: www.pen-and-sword.co.uk

# Contents

For All

Old Braggs and Slashers

Who

For 300 Years

Served Crown and Country

In

Peace and War

# Preface

'If it can be said that any man enjoyed the Great War, that man was Brigadier-General Pagan.' So wrote Lieutenant General Wetherall, Pagan's successor as Colonel of the Gloucestershire Regiment, in a telling summary of his four years of unbroken service on the Western Front from January 1915 to October 1918. His record must be unparalleled. For three of the four years he commanded the 1st Battalion the Gloucestershire Regiment in some of the bitterest fighting of that bloody war. For the remainder he was either a company or brigade commander.

The vast majority of commanding officers were either killed, wounded, promoted, or moved to an instructional school, or to the Staff. The latter Pagan was able to avoid because he had not attended the Army Staff College at Camberley, nor did he have any interest in becoming a staff learner. It was not that he despised the Staff – although he could be as scathing as a subaltern about 'fat majors at the Base' – indeed, he was complimentary about their efforts on behalf of his men. But to pursue any of these possible paths would have meant leaving his battalion, his beloved 28th, and this he was determined to avoid. The officers of the 2/5th Gloucesters, an excellent Territorial battalion which he was privileged to have under his command when later he was directed, much against his wishes, to take over 184 Brigade, summed him up accurately: the new brigadier, they said, had a heart like a lion, and two interests in life, the Gloucestershire Regiment and Rugby football.

In many ways, then, Alexander William Pagan exemplified the ideal regimental soldier of one hundred years ago. It is humbling for us, of later generations, to recognise how complete was this dedication to a regiment and its men, how deep ran his wish to identify himself with every aspect, and how entire was his knowledge not just of his men's backgrounds. He even knew their regimental numbers. His book, *Infantry*, produced in instalments in the regimental journal, *The Back Badge*, but not published in book form until after his death, is a remarkable record. Almost unique – the only other work by a regular commanding officer over a similar period, *The Land Locked Lake*, is rather mystical, and concerned more with the feelings of its author, Hanbury-Tennyson of the Royal Berkshire Regiment, than with the practical affairs of his command – *Infantry* tells in a straight-forward, almost laconic, fashion of the way in which a regular battalion of infantry conducted itself throughout one of the most trying times in the history of the British Army.

Pagan's attitude to the war is summed up in the words that may be found in the Epilogue, which begin, 'Service with a good infantry battalion in France was the highest thing attainable during the years 1914 to 1918.' He was immensely proud to have played the part that he did. He was not blind to, nor disinterested in, the unpleasant aspects of trench life. The discomfort and sheer nastiness are well recognised. Nor does he shrink from acknowledging the huge casualties that were suffered. But his way of dealing with them was to see them as a personal challenge to his regiment – and he was the best man to confront that challenge. In doing so he was awarded the DSO and two foreign decorations, mentioned five times in despatches, and wounded three times: on the first occasion he was able to remain at duty; on the second he had to be hospitalised in England for two months; on the third, about to be evacuated again, he discharged himself from medical care and made his way, in dressing gown and canvas shoes, back to the 28th. For this, and for the attitude which it exemplified, he became a legend within the regiment, a legend which persisted long after his death. After the war, when he visited the Bristol Aeroplane Company at Filton, work came to a standstill as his old soldiers left their benches and desks to catch a glimpse of him.

Sadly, once he relinquished command of the 28th in March 1918, life never held the same satisfaction. The huge cuts in the post-war army reduced prospects, and with no Staff qualification, Pagan was fortunate to retain his acting rank of brigadier for a year, before losing it and returning to regimental duty – but not as commanding officer; that coveted appointment was to remain beyond his grasp for the remainder of his career. His retirement in 1929, soon followed by appointment as Colonel of the Regiment, enabled him to immerse himself in regimental affairs, but without the influence which those more fortunate could expect from one of higher rank, and of the brotherhood of Camberley. The outbreak of the Second World War appeared to offer more useful employment, and Pagan threw himself whole heartedly into his work with the Home Guard and a Young Soldiers Battalion. But the many tribulations of service life at his age, and in a backwater, his failing health, and the vicissitudes to which the regiment was subjected, became an increasing burden.

This book tells the story of 'Patsy' Pagan's life, in a series of vignettes, which portray not only the man, but also the regiment. Under the Cardwell reforms of the late nineteenth century, the old regiments of foot were linked firmly to their county affiliations. So, the 28th Foot became the First Battalion, and the 61st the Second Battalion, of the Gloucestershire Regiment, but for many years both were referred to by their former titles. The 3rd, or Militia Battalion became the Special Reserve, a training cadre for men and officers, and the 4th, 5th and 6th Battalions were Territorials. With the expansion of the army in 1914, further battalions were raised; thus the 2/5th was a Second Line Territorial battalion, and the 10th a New Army unit. They are spelled in many different ways, as are other units and other entities, from machine guns to mortars, in the official documents which form part of the text, and no attempt has been made to rationalise this usage. Staff duties, over which much red ink is now spilled, were in their infancy over the period of this book, and illustrious regiments such as the Oxford and Buckinghamshire Light Infantry, or the Ox and Bucks as they came to be known, were referred to as 'the Oxfords.' War diaries were written by the adjutant at battalion level, or staff captain at brigade level in difficult conditions and much danger; to read them in their original format is to relive those stern days, and the text has been left unaltered deliberately in an attempt to invoke that era.

This book is also the story of the Gloucestershire Regiment, and of the British Army, from the Boer War – in which a newly commissioned Lieutenant Pagan found himself commanding a company under fire for the first time – through peacetime, to the British Expeditionary Force in France, to Ireland on the brink of revolution, to peacetime soldiering at home and in the Empire. The Gloucesters as a regiment are no more. In three hundred years of loyal service, they won more battle honours on their regimental colour than any other regiment, and gained the unique distinction of the Back Badge for their courage at the Battle of Alexandria in 1801. After passing through numerous transitions, occasioned by changing defence priorities, they came to their present status as one of the 'antecedent regiments' of the Rifles.

The book takes as its viewpoint the regular soldier, and his life, and sadly so often his death. The chances of a regular army officer surviving the First War were one in ten, and for soldiers little different; there were therefore few left to tell the tale, and when they did, as Pagan did, few members of the public were inclined to listen. The one hundredth anniversary of that conflict gives us the opportunity to assess anew the experiences of those who took part. History has not been kind to the leaders of the nation, or of the British army, in the greatest conflict the world had ever seen until the second, even greater, catastrophe. The politicians are criticised for not avoiding the conflict, and for poor strategy, the generals for unimaginative tactics and a callous disregard for human life. Such critics will find little to strengthen their case here. Pagan is generous in his praise for his divisional and brigade commanders, as he is for any of the regiment who advanced its cause. Of Lieutenant Colonel Lawson, of the 11th Hussars, who became a byword for courage as commanding officer of the 2/5th Gloucesters, he said, 'This officer was only approached by one other as a battalion commander among the many I met in France. He was absolutely fearless, very able, and was devoted to the welfare of his men. He was always unruffled, whatever the circumstances, and was a very fine leader of men.' These words could be used to describe Pagan himself.

In all the literature of the war, it is rare to find an understanding of either the difficulties, or the potential for destruction, of warfare in the industrial age, in which the means of taking life exceeded the ability to control events to an unprecedented degree.

Two factors dominated events: artillery and communications. Critics, such as C S Forester in *The General*, pour scorn on the commanders' obsession with the need for more and heavier guns to fire more and greater shells prior to an attack. Yet in the offensive of March 1918, it was precisely because they were able to concentrate such devastating artillery fire on the British lines, for almost the first time in the war by either side, that the Germans were able to make such headway. To be truly effective, artillery relies on good communication, to enable fire to be adjusted as a changing situation demands. But communication, command and control, and information, were to remain the defining lacunae in the tactics of all participants throughout the conflict.

Wellington at Waterloo could view the entire battlefield from his horse. If he required a unit to carry out a particular manoeuvre he could send a galloper to a commander on the spot; he in turn could use his voice to carry out the commander's wishes. In the Boer War, engagements were fought by relatively small formations, again largely commanded by voice, but coordinated across a vast area by telegraph and heliograph. The First World War imposed different limitations. Across a frontage of over one hundred miles, with an army of between one and two million men, command could be assured to a limited extent by telephone, or even primitive radio. But this system only held good from GHQ to Army, to Corps and down to Division. Below that level, radios were too bulky and immobile, and telephone lines, even when dug into the ground, liable to be cut. But neither the general commanding the fifteen thousand men of his division, nor the brigadier general commanding the three to four thousand of his brigade, could command by voice, and even the commanding officer of a battalion of eight hundred to one thousand men was hard put to control events in person.

A series of drills, known as Battle Procedure, could enable a plan, hatched by the politicians, refined and detailed at the intervening stages by commanders and staffs, to be communicated to, and prepared for implementation by, the units involved. Orders could be given, reconnaissance carried out, march and artillery time tables prepared, men and guns moved into position, supplies and reinforcements and medical plans prepared in huge detail, and preparatory operations, be it mining or artillery barrage, begun. But, from the moment the men went over the top, control was effectively lost. Plans could be made, but as the old adage goes, no plan survives contact with the enemy. Every possible expedient was tried: letter and display boards to be shown above a trench to mark a unit's position, flares to call down emergency artillery support, pigeons, runners, all were experimented with. Lieutenant Colonel Tweedie, who succeeded Pagan in command of the 28th, observed, about the Battle of Festubert, 'Long ere this stage had been reached all telephonic communications had been cut, and we were dependent on our own runners, a picked body of men who may have been equalled but never surpassed for gallantry or sustained devotion to duty.' Indeed, the note in one of the Operation Orders quoted, that dead or wounded runners should be searched for their message, which should be carried onwards with the utmost determination, tells its own story. This problem lay behind the dilemma faced by every battalion commander: where to place himself in battle.

The casualties suffered in the first months of the war, not least by generals, over one hundred and fifty of whom were eventually to be killed, and by those of lesser rank qualified to command formations and units, forced the British Army, no doubt against its own better instincts, to issue orders that limited the exposure of commanding officers. Fine words, but they did not solve the problem. A CO who stuck to the letter, and remained to the rear, risked the failure of his operation. A CO who led from the front, as Pagan always did, risked death. Thus it was that so many commanding officers died or were seriously wounded, and thus it is that 'Patsy' Pagan's record of four years continuous service at the front, is so extraordinary. For this alone, his story is worth the telling.

To add atmosphere to the narrative, I have included passages in italics which, while recording accurately basic facts, contain material, such as the detail of conversations, which are conjectural. In researching this book, I owe a great debt to Rob Dixon and The Soldiers of Gloucestershire Museum, and particularly the archivist, David Read, who has been unfailingly helpful and generous in allowing me to use its records; the

# Preface

Museum and the Tailyour family for permission to draw heavily on Pagan's own writing; the National Archives, Kew; the Military Secretary's Department; the Gutenberg Press; Cheltenham College, in particular their Archive Department; Gerald Napier; many members of the regimental family, and particularly Mark Lavender, and his father, John, descendants of a famous officer of the regiment, Christopher Newbould, Claud Rebbeck and Jill Arengo-Jones; the people of Upton St Leonards, Gloucester; those few who knew Pagan personally and have added immeasurably to my understanding; and to my wife and family for their unfailing encouragement and support.

Peter Rostron
Abbeydore 2014

# Prologue

*January fog and engine smoke blur the outlines of the station. Figures that were in sharp relief close up become ill-defined a few paces away. One colour prevails. Although the odd dark blue spots the crowd, khaki has been the predominant colour at this London terminus for four months. The soldiers move in groups that coalesce and then diffuse. Older men and women, wives, sweethearts, children, cling and break away. There are the bright eyes of expectation, a sense of adventure, of the unknown, of honour attended. There are other eyes; the eyes of experience, of duty fulfilled, of knowing.*

*He moves purposely through the crowd of departing men and their well wishers. No family for him, he has said his goodbyes to Mother and sisters, there is no more to be said. It is his calling, and he is glad to go. Impatient, he has been willing this move for four months, to fulfil his destiny, to play his part, to be with his regiment. He is a professional soldier, he knows the roar of artillery, the crackle of rifle fire, the sights, the sounds, the smells of the battle field, and he has the confidence of the initiate.*

*He locates the Rail Transport Officer, his professional sense of decorum mollified to find a young captain of a Rifle regiment. His empty sleeve and scarred cheek reassure that he is no dugout in an easy billet. 'One Div? First carriage – when you get to Folkestone look for the Port Arthur.'*

*The train is full, over full, his compartment crowded, pipe and cigarette smoke thicken the air. His companions identify themselves: 'Munsters', 'South Wales Borderers', 'Welsh Regiment.' He speaks proudly: 'Gloucesters'. The senior officer present, a thickset major of the Queen's Surreys, speaks of Mons. 'The papers don't seem to understand, we only withdrew because the French on our right had pulled back.' A Gunner tells of the frustration of shell shortage, a Sapper of the difficulties of communication once an assault begins, another the difficulty of draining trenches knee deep in water. The men are all regulars, the air one of calm judgement. The exception is a subaltern from the Militia, a stockbroker until a few months ago. He asks about casualties. The regulars reassure him; they do not know that nine out of ten of their cohort will be dead by the time the business is settled.*

*The Channel crossing is now a memory, his train less comfortable. The Normandy countryside slides by, the sodden fields, the small villages where no young men abide. They are received without fanfare – the bands and flags of last August are a distant memory. At Bethune, the train shudders to a halt, and another RTO directs him towards a waiting lorry. A sergeant with an extra crown on his sleeve is at attention. 'Orderly Room Sergeant, Sir, Brasington, I was asked to meet you, I could tell you were one of us when I saw the cap badges. The Battalion is at Givenchy, Battalion HQ is on the south bank of the canal. I won't come up the line with you now Sir, but you will see me when the next big show is on.'*

*At 3 Brigade Echelon he is met by the Regimental Quartermaster Sergeant, Hague, an old friend from South Africa days, where he served with the 1st Battalion. Hague is going forward with the rations, and the two reminisce as the lorry jerks forward. The sights and sounds of war are all around them now. They pass gun lines where the occasional 13 or 18 pounder fires, horse lines, a RAMC field dressing station, supply dumps. The rumble of German artillery is loud enough to be heard above the harsh racket of the lorry.*

*'Here you are Sir, Battalion Headquarters.' He jumps down and collects his kit from the back of the lorry. Beside the sign saying 28th, a burly figure appears out of the evening gloom, a large coat of arms the only rank badge on his sleeve. An immaculate salute is thrown, and a deep voice drowns the sounds of battle. 'Captain Pagan? RSM Brain, Sir. Welcome Home'*

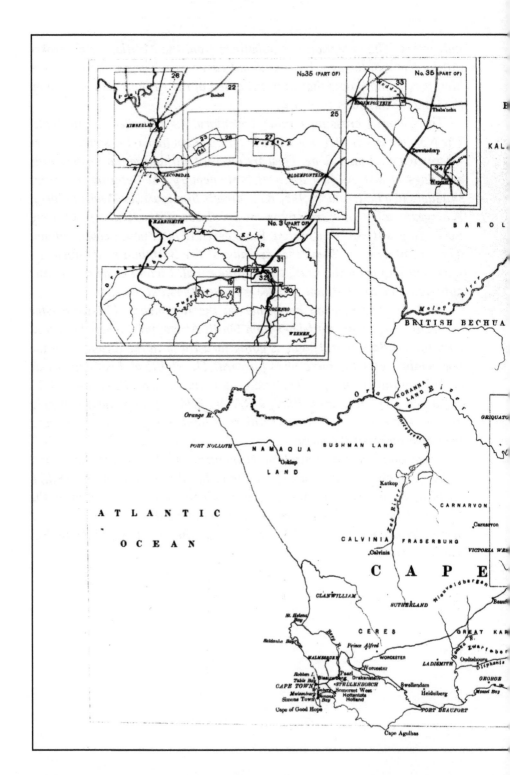

# Chapter 1

'Why do the bells ring so, Mama? Why do the bells ring so?'

'It is the Jubilee of our dear Queen, Alexander, she has been Queen and Empress for fifty years. Cheltenham is celebrating.'

'And why are the soldiers marching, Mama, where are they going?'

'It is the Volunteers, Alexander, see how smart they look in their green coats.'

'Soldiers should wear red, I have seen pictures of them.'

'Those are the proper soldiers, the regulars. These are the gentlemen soldiers.'

'I want to be a soldier and wear a red coat.'

'What a funny idea, Alexander, I am sure you will change your mind when you grow up. You are only nine.'

'Mother, please show me the medal.'

'The medal, Alexander, do you mean grandpa Samuel's medal?'

'Yes, Mother, the medal he won for being so brave.'

'It is the Waterloo medal, all the soldiers who fought that day were given the medal. He always said it took a long time to come, but better late than never.'

'I like the blue and red of the ribbon. Was Grandpa in the Gloucestershire Regiment?'

'No, Dear, he was in the 33rd Foot. That is now the Duke of Wellington's Regiment; they all come from Yorkshire. Look, here is the framed letter which he wrote to your great grandmother after the battle.'

'Mama, now that I am sixteen, I should like to talk about what I am going to do when I leave Cheltenham. I should like to be a soldier. My house master, Doctor Macgowan, says that I would make a good soldier, and the Sergeant said last Corps day that I had the makings of a proper *officer. He was in the Engineers, what they call the Sappers, but he knows all about the Gloucestershire Regiment, our local regiment, you know. They wear two cap badges, one at the front and one at the back. He says they have more battle honours on their Regimental Colour than any other regiment.'*

*'I expect your Sergeant is like all the rest, drinking too much and not fit for decent company. You must think of Ethilda and Violet – if you go away who will look after them? Now that your dear Father is gone, I have to think of the future.'*

*'I am going for a soldier, Mama.'*

*A chill autumn day in Surrey. A listless wind corrals the dead leaves and manoeuvres them into small heaps around the parade ground. In front of the imposing white facade of the College building a large man is addressing a group of 100 or so young men.*

*'Now all you young gentlemen listen to me. I am Sergeant Major Lambton, and I will be your Company Sergeant Major for your first term at The Royal Military College. I belong to the First or Grenadier Regiment of Foot Guards, the senior infantry regiment in the Army, and do not forget it. I want to make one thing clear. I call you Sir, and you call me Sir. The difference is, you mean it, I don't. Your fathers have paid a lot of money to send you here, and for the next two years you should show that you are worth it. We will teach you to drill to the highest standard in the Army. We will teach you how to drill each other. We will teach you the care of arms and equipment, we will teach you military history, and we will teach you how to behave on the field of battle. Most important, we will teach you how to live like an officer and a gentleman, and, God help us, how to die like one. Is that clear?'*

*'Yes Sir!'*

# Chapter 1

*An officer sits at his desk. Regimental regalia proclaim his allegiance, a crown on his cuff that he is the commander of No 2 Company of the Royal Military College, Sandhurst. Loud noises beyond his office door herald the entry of Sergeant Major Lambton, who comes heavily to attention in front of the desk.*

'Gentleman Cadet Pagan, Sir.'

'Have a pew, Pagan. You are due to commission in a few weeks?'

'Yes, Sir.'

'Into the Gloucestershire Regiment?'

'Yes, Sir.'

Yes, the old Fore and Afts. Two cap badges,eh? Fine regiment, knew them in India – First Battalion of course. Now, the point is, which battalion for you? The old 28th are at Allahabad, the 61st in the Channel Isles, but warned for Aldershot soon.'

*The major fiddles with papers on his desk, hesitant, unsure how to approach his next point.*

'The thing is, Pagan, between ourselves....you see the point is....dammit, in India a young officer can live off his pay, little enough though it is. In England...'

*He trails off, uncertain.*

'I do understand, Sir, one needs money of one's own to live in England. I think I shall be able to manage.'

'Father was a sheep farmer I see. Many sheep?'

'About forty thousand I believe. He farmed in New Zealand. He left Mother well provided for. I would be very happy to go to the 61st.'

'That settles it then, you should have a jolly time in Aldershot. They are beginning to call it the Home of the British Army. Good hunting, and plenty of time for poodle faking if that is your line of country. Yes, it should be ripping.....if those goddam Boers don't make too much trouble...'

'To our trusty and well beloved servant, Alexander William Pagan, Greetings.....to be a Second Lieutenant of Land Forces in the Gloucestershire Regiment.......dated 11th February 1899 ...................................**Victoria Regina et Imperatrix**.'

**Extract from a speech by Sir Alfred Milner, High Commissioner for South Africa and Governor of Cape Colony, 12 June 1899**

'The principle of equality of races is essential for the whole of South Africa. The one state where inequality exists keeps all the others in a fever. Our policy is not one of aggression, but of singular patience, which cannot, however, lapse into indifference.'

**Extract from a speech by President Kruger of the Transvaal Republic, 14 June 1899**

The other side has not conceded one tittle, and I could not give away more. God has always stood by us. I do not want war, but I will not give more away.'

**Despatch from Sir Arthur Milner, July 1899**

'The spectacle of thousands of British subjects kept permanently in the position of helots, constantly chafing under undoubted grievances, and calling vainly to Her Majesty's Government for redress, does steadily undermine the influence and reputation of Great Britain within the Queen's dominions.'

**Message received from the Cape at the Colonial Office, 6 September 1899**

The present strength of British Forces in South Africa amounts to approximately 6,000 men. Against these, it is estimated that the Boer states could put in the field forty or fifty thousand mounted riflemen, supported by the most modern artillery from Krupps and Creusot. I am informed by the General Officer Commanding Natal that he will not have enough troops, even when the

# Chapter 1

Manchester Regiment arrives, to do more than occupy Newcastle and protect the south from raids... the Boers have made up their minds that war will take place almost certainly, and that their best chance will be to deliver a blow before our reinforcements arrive.

**Message from the British Government to Pretoria, 8 September 1899**

'Assuming acceptance of the condition of the five years 'franchise', and assuming that in the Raad each member may talk his own language... Acceptance of these terms by the South African Republic would at once remove tension... and secure redress for grievances which the Uitlanders themselves would be able to bring to... the Executive Council and the Volksraad.'

'We have beaten England before, but it is nothing to the licking we shall give her now.'

*The Officers' Mess. 2nd Battalion Gloucestershire regiment (61st Foot), Aldershot, Hampshire, 1 October 1899.*

*'I say Colonel, here's a go! The jolly old 28th are for the Cape! It says in the Times that the Berkshires, Munster Fusiliers, Manchesters, Dublin Fusiliers, Devons, Rifle Corps and Gordons are with them, and they will land at Durban on the 13th. That should show old Kruger. But what about us? When do we go?'*

*Colonel Lindsell smiles.*

*'You know what the old hands say – never be in command or in the field when the British Army begins a war. Things go wrong, politicians look for scapegoats, and soldiers take the casualties and the blame for the failings of the frocks.'*

*This is as close as the Commanding Officer is likely to come to breaching the old adage that one should never discuss politics, religion or women in the Mess.*

*'Mark my words, young Pagan, we will all have a turn before this business with the Boers is settled. You keep up the good work with D Company, and keep your powder dry.'*

### Ultimatum from the Boer Government to the British Government, 9 October 1899

'All British troops upon the borders should be instantly withdrawn, all reinforcements which have arrived within the last year should leave South Africa, those upon the sea should turn back. Failing a satisfactory answer within forty-eight hours, the Transvaal overnment will be compelled to regard the action of Her Majesty's Government as a formal declaration of war...'

### Reply by the British Government, 10 October 1899

'Her Majesty's Government have received with great regret the peremptory demands of the Government of the Transvaal... the conditions are such as Her Majesty's Government deem it impossible to discuss.'

*Aldershot, Hampshire, 4 November 1899*

*'Gentlemen, I have the gravest possible news. The 28th, as you know, were moved to Ladysmith as soon as they landed in South Africa. They have been in action at a place called Rietfontein, but a few days later they were involved in an awful business at Nicolson's Nek, just outside the city. During a night move the supply train bolted, and several companies were cut off.'*

*Here Colonel Lindsell seems unable to speak. He scans the official communique anxiously, seeking reassurance, finding none.*

# Chapter 1

'The fact is....the fact is that several officers and some hundreds of men from the 28th are now prisoners of the Boers, and the remainder of the Battalion are shut up in Ladysmith until such time as General Buller can relieve them. I have of course wired to the Rear Party in Allahabad a message of such encouragement as I could offer, but we must face the fact that this is a difficult moment for the Regiment.'

The Colonel is being tactful, even evasive. The assembled officers know this. There is incomprehension, a shifting of seats, a low growl of anger spreading through the room. Every officer is keen to reverse this affront, to wipe clean this stain upon their escutcheon. Then the announcement they long for.

'However, I am assured by General Kelly-Kenny that, should reinforcement be called for from England, the whole of the 6th Division will be the first to go. We, as part of General Knox's 12th Brigade with the Oxfords, the West Ridings and the Buffs, will be at the forefront. I regard this as an order to prepare for war. Gentlemen, swords and bayonets should be sharpened.'

The Laurels
Saint Stephen Road
Cheltenham
20 December 1899

Dear Alexander

Christmas is upon us, and it will be so strange this year not to have you with us. The girls are so disappointed, as am I, but of course you must do your duty. I am so glad you were able to spend a few days with us, as I know you leave shortly, and the Good Lord only knows when we shall see you again. We pray for a quick end to this silly war, and hope that this man Kruger will soon see sense.

You probably know that the papers have been calling the latest reverses Black Week, and we feel so sorry for the poor men who have been killed and wounded. We seemed to be doing so well at Belmont and Graspan, but then the reverses at Stormberg and then Magersfontein and Colenso came as a heavy blow. You see that I am becoming accustomed to these strange names! Vi has them all marked on a map she is keeping with little flags for our brave forces.

*We understand that the men of the 28th who were taken prisoner are well cared for, and held in a school in Pretoria. Effie and I helped at the Pump Rooms yesterday. We were packing parcels with a few comforts for them, with dear Mrs Lindsell – she, poor thing, is totally blind, as you know, and could not see a thing.*

*The Times says that you will be at the Cape in late January, so I am sending this ahead of you to greet you at Aden. It comes with our dearest love, we pray every day for your safety.*

*Your loving Mother*

### Report by Lieutenant Salvage,
### 2nd Battalion Gloucestershire Regiment

The 61st moved out from Salamanca Barracks, Aldershot, at dawn on the morning of the 24th December 1899. It was a real winter's morning with the snow many feet deep. Entraining for Liverpool, where the White Star liner *Olympic* awaited our arrival, we embarked the same day, Christmas Eve, together with artillery units and hundreds of horses destined for the front to replace casualties.

On Christmas Day, before sailing, we were treated to a sumptuous feast which seemed too good to last. We left Liverpool during the night, fully expecting ham and eggs for breakfast next morning, roast beef and plum pudding for dinner, and so on. But what a rude awakening was in store – bully beef, salt pork and ship's biscuits was all we got for the next 21 days.

Inoculation against typhoid or enteric fever followed, and most of the lads were rendered hors de combat for a few hours in consequence. The voyage was extremely rough, and for some days we were battened down; altogether we lost seven men and some 400 horses, from one cause or another, between Liverpool and Cape Town. Disembarking at Cape Town we entrained for De Aar. On arrival there will forms were issued with instructions to complete before going into action. No more trains or cattle-truck journeys were made after this for many months.

# Chapter 1

We formed part of a brigade under General Charles Knox, serving with the famous 6th Division, under the command of General Kenny-Kenny of 'tread on the tail of my coat' fame. Lord Roberts (Bobs) had by this time taken over supreme command of the South African Forces, with Lord Kitchener as second in command.

*From a letter home by an officer of the 61st, 10 February 1900*

*'Here we are at Modder. On the evening of Wednesday 31st January we heard we were to move, but not told where. Trains full of men came passing through and next day we entrained and as we pushed on we realised we were for the Modder. The Regiment is very fit now but none of our stores have come up from Capetown. This is a very hot place, no shade, burning sun all day and even worse by night. This appears to be a beastly country, nothing more than a sandy desert covered by scrub.*

*We are jolly lucky to have got up here, it is evidently going to be a big thing. We fire a few shells at the Boers every morning and evening and they return the compliment but our camp is well out of range. We expect to move quite soon, the hope is to catch a large force of Boers under Cronje.*

*It is good to be serving under Lord Roberts (Bobs or Bobs Bahadur as the old India hands call him). He gives us such a feeling of confidence.'*

**Digest of Services. 2nd Battalion Gloucestershire Regiment**

**12-2-00. Marched at 3-30 am as Advanced Guard. At about 9 am arrived at Ram Dam**
**13-2-00. Marched at daybreak. Arrived at Watervaal Drift at 1-30 pm. This was a very trying march owing to the heat and lack of water.**
**14-2-00. Marched at about 6 pm. At about 1 am a halt was made, after marching about 15 miles in a heavy thunderstorm, and the men slept as well as they could without blankets or coats. Total distance marched – 30 miles in 24 hours.**
**15-2-00. General French moved out with his cavalry division on his march to relieve Kimberley.**

**16-2-00. The Brigade moved out at 3-30 am, the Buffs leading, followed by the Gloucesters, as it was reported that Cronje was trekking from Magersfontein towards Bloemfontein, having only just discovered that Lord Roberts' Army was advancing. The Artillery came into action at about 6 am. Soon afterwards the Battalion came under fire for the first time in the war.**

*'Can you tell where the firing is coming from, Colour Sergeant?'*

*'No Sir, but I can tell where it's coming to', replies 'Lakri' Wood, eighteen years service, much of it in India. The Boers are obviously in some strength, judging from the volume of fire, but it is almost impossible to make out individual targets. The veldt is green, the grass high enough to conceal a man on his belly. The Boers have been wily enough to wait until the rains have readied grazing for their ponies, before they declare war.*

*He can distinguish the 'crack', as the bullet sings past, from the 'thump' of the cartridge being fired, just like the demonstration in the butts at Sandhurst. The men are returning fire now, sights at 1,000 yards, the solid thud of their Lee-Metfords responding to the waspish sound of the Mausers, English men against Dutch, West country boys against Transvaal farmers.*

*His mind casts back over the last twenty four hours; the whispered orders passed from tent to tent in the middle of the night; the noiseless move out in the darkness, leaving the camp in position; the short rations. The men have done well. They grumble about the one hard biscuit and a quarter that is their day's lot, but they march well, keen to catch the enemy.*

*He is proud of his command, he had not expected to be leading a company so soon, but the fortunes of war, and the illness of Captain Whylock, have given him early responsibility. He remembers again the Colonel's praise after yesterday's march, and the gruff 'Well done, Mister Pagan, Sir' of RSM Trevelyan.*

# Chapter 1

Digest of Services. 2nd Battalion Gloucestershire Regiment

16-2-00. After about two hours heavy firing the enemy were driven from their first position, and retired to a long line of kopjes, with very open ground in front. The Gloucesters then advanced with the intention of turning the enemy's right flank... A brisk fire was maintained by both sides until 4 pm, when the whole line again advanced. When within about 700 yards of the position, darkness came on, and the attack was ordered to cease. During the night, the enemy, who were evidently the rearguard of the main Boer force, withdrew. The Battalion passed a very cold night without food, coats or blankets.

17-2-00. The Battalion marched at 5-30 am. With two halts, of about 30 minutes each, the Battalion marched to a point close to Paardeberg Drift, about 25miles.

18-2-00. At 4-30 am news was received that, owing to our rapid marching, Cronje's Army was overtaken and was encamped on the Modder River a few miles ahead. At about 6-30 am the guns opened fire, but the Battalion did not take part in the first part of the fight. At 3 pm, however, a force under De Wet captured a kopje, afterwards known as Kitchener's Kopje, on the right flank of the Division. The Battalion was sent to prevent them from advancing further. Positions were taken up, and the Battalion entrenched about 1,300 yards from the enemy. Fire was exchanged by both sides and continued until dark.

19-2-00. At daybreak the Boers were still in position on the kopje, and opened a hot fire throughout the day. In the afternoon, orders were received to take the Boer position. A large number of men were getting water for their comrades, which they had been without for 24 hours. Thus the total number attacking the position, which was held by about 700 Boers, was only about 350. The following Companies took part in the attack: 'B' Company, under Major Richardson-Griffiths, 'C' Company under Capt Moss, 'D' Company under Lieut Pagan... The men advanced steadily in extended order till within about 800 yards of the position, when the advance was made by individual rushes, the remainder of the line covering the advance. The Maxim Gun detachment, under Lieut Wethered, covered the advance by firing over the heads of the Battalion from a good position 1,300 yards from the enemy. Just as it was getting dark, a charge with the bayonet was made, and the whole of the position, except a small kopje on the left, was taken. The casualties during this engagement were five men killed, and Lieut Colonel Lindsell , Lieut Harington and 19 men wounded. Col. Lindsell was shot through the lungs before the charge, but in spite of this he led his men to the top of the kopje, a most gallant act. Colonel the Hon Dalyell, who commanded the force, said 'The Gloucesters worked uncommonly well, and got up in spite of a pretty heavy fire, and the Boers retired.'

*Paardeberg*
*26 February 1900*

*Dear Mother*
*I am as you see still here, and I suppose likely to be unless Cronje surrenders or manages to escape some time. We have absolutely surrounded them, but I should not think it is very hard to get through in twos and threes on a dark night. I think take it all round the Boers are bad shots, but have a few particularly good ones.*
*We supply NCOs every night for outpost duties, and the weather has been awful, heavy thunderstorms and rain by the hour. Last night I was sent out on a vile fatigue from 5 to 12 midnight with 100 men to dig the siege trenches up to the Boer position. We were about 700 yards from their position, but what made it so bad was the stench of dead men and horses. There are scores of dead horses floating down the river, which sounds bad for our drinking supply. What the Boer laager is like I can't think but judging from the stench last night it must be awful. The men have been on half rations since we have been here and grumble a good deal though there is plenty of meat.*
*We have had some of the Pom Poms sent up to us, and as I write they are bringing up siege guns 6". It takes 16 oxen to draw one gun.*

# Chapter 1

*Great things have happened since I started this letter. Just after the siege guns passed we got orders that the Brigade was to take up a position on the South side of the river, as spies brought in word that the Boers intended to bolt in that direction. No one was allowed to sleep, we shelled the Boers during the night, and the IX Div fired heavy musketry into them. Next morning we got news that Cronje had surrendered unconditionally, and we now have 4,000 prisoners to guard.*

*We escorted the prisoners to Klipkraal Drift. I have never seen such a sight. They were ragged, patched, grotesque, some with goloshes, some with umbrellas, coffee pots and Bibles – their favourite baggage. The blacks all jeered at the Boer prisoners as we marched them away. I am not at all surprised as the Boers treat the Kaffirs very badly.*

*The turn around in the fortunes of war is remarkable. A few days ago Kimberley was in danger of capture, a victorious Boer army was facing Methuen, Clements was being pressed at Coolesberg, and we were in dire straits at Stormberg, the Tugela and Ladysmith. Now Kimberley is relieved, elsewhere the Boer is in retreat, with Gatacre advancing on Stormberg, and Ladysmith should be relieved soon.*

*Today we marched to Osfontein Farm, as we were getting so many sick from the bad water in the Modder. I wonder we are not all sick as the water is the colour of tar and full of dead horses.*

*Now we are getting beautiful water and a much nicer camp. The men are all very pleased with the telegrams from the Queen, Prince of Wales, etc. Best love to all.*

*Your affec son*
*Alexander*

Digest of Service of 2nd Battalion Gloucestershire Regiment

7-3-00. Marched at 2-30 am. The enemy were reported to be holding a position at Poplar Grove. The 6th Division, preceded by the Cavalry and the Mounted Infantry, were ordered to turn the enemy's left flank. The position was about 14 miles long, and the enemy reported to be 8,000 to 14,000 strong. The enemy however fled, before the mounted troops succeeded in cutting off their retreat. The Battalion marched all day up to 7 pm when they arrived at Poplar Grove. The total distance marched was about 30 miles.

10-3-00. Marched at 5-30 am for Driefontein. At about 11 am, after about a 12 mile march, heavy artillery firing was heard in front. The 18th Brigade was leading followed by the Buffs and then the Gloucesters. The other two Battalions of the Brigade were escorting the convoy. At about 1 pm the Battalion came under a heavy cross shell fire, but the men advanced steadily through it. The 18th Brigade then advanced to the attack, supported by the Buffs and the Gloucesters. The Battalion was under a heavy cross fire, both of Artillery and Musketry throughout the day. Towards evening two companies were ordered to reinforce the firing line, one of which took part in the final charge on the Boer position, and suffered severely. Most of the night was spent in collecting the dead and wounded.

14-3-00. The Brigade marched at 10 am to Bloemfontein. Lord Roberts inspected the troops as they passed through Maitland Street. The men presented a most dilapidated appearance, their clothes in many cases being nearly worn off their backs. Thus ended the most brilliant march of the war, successful from start to finish, and the turning point of the campaign.

# Chapter 1

*Bloemfontein*
*15 March 1900*

*Dear Mother*

*Well, we are in Bloemfontein, and I think as far as the Free Staters are concerned we shall have no more trouble. First we had the affairs at Poplar Grove, then at Driefontein. At the former the Boers had taken up a position extended across the Modder River, and was reinforced with guns, rifle pits and barbed wire. Lord Roberts was too clever to get mixed up with this, so set upon an outflanking movement – fortunately or unfortunately, the Boer sensed this and slipped away. Our part in this action was to march like mad! The second, at Driefontein or Abram's Kraal, was a real dog fight. The whole of our Division was involved in assaulting the position, which stretched for a good seven miles. The Welsh, the Buffs and the Essex had the worst of it, but we also lost four killed and twenty wounded. Moss and Harington did splendidly, and are both up for a mention.*

*On the 13th we did not parade until 5.30 pm and did not get to camp till 2.30 am on 14th. We did escort to a convoy and had a miserable night, as the convoy kept stopping, and there was a steady downpour of rain from about 8 till 12 and again when we got into camp. I had only a thin flannel shirt under my khaki and of course was soaked through, and when we got into camp, we had to lie down as we were, the blankets not having arrived; however I slept all right and am none the worse.*

*The next morning we paraded at 6 am and marched the 8 miles into Bloemfontein. It is a small town with a few good buildings and houses rather like the new ones in Painswick. The few inhabitants who were left, mostly English, turned out and cheered us. Poor people they have had a poor time from the Boers lately. The Boers made no fight here. We are in camp and close to the town. It is good to see the Union Jack flying here. I fancy we shall be here two or three weeks. Our job will be to send out columns to scour the countryside for the small bands or 'commandos' of Boers that remain in this part.*

*Yr affec son*
*Alexander*

**Digest of Service of 2nd Battalion Gloucestershire Regiment**

1-4-00. Marched at daybreak. Spent the day skirmishing over the kopjes near the river, to try and get information on the enemy.

20-4-00. Changed camp to a place about 4 miles west of the town. This was due to the Battalion having suffered severely from enteric fever. Officers and men were going sick from this cause daily, and funerals were an almost daily occurrence.

1-5-00. 2nd Lieut. Noel, who had only recently joined the regiment returned to Bloemfontein with enteric fever and died shortly afterwards.

10-6-00. B and C Companies left on a flying column for Thabanchu and returned on the 21st inst.

4-10-00. A, B and F companies under Major Tufnell left Bloemfontein for Dewetsdorp.

*'I say, Pagan, have you heard the news? Major Tufnell has run into a bit of trouble at Dewetsdorp. His men were part of a force that was attacked by De Wet with about 1,700 men. They held out for three days but in the end they had no chance, and had to surrender. Apparently Foord behaved absolutely splendidly, and Major Tufnell was commended by the column commander for the men's performance. It seems we lost 10 killed and about 30 wounded. Wingfield-Digby is one, but no one knows how bad.'*

*'Bad news. But I would not lay odds on De Wet hanging on to them for too long. He's being chased pretty hard, and they will just slow him down. I wager you we shall see their cheery faces before long.'*

**Digest of Service of 2nd Battalion Gloucestershire Regiment**

9-12-00. Had a brush with the Boers near Welte Verde. Killed one, took 4 prisoners and captured 15 horses and some arms, ammunition and saddlery.

19-12-00. Marched west at 5-30 am and halted at Brak River (17 miles)

**20-12-00. Marched at 4-30 am and halted at Pampoenpoort (17 miles)**
**24-12-00. Marched to Kaffir Kraal (17 miles)**
**01-1-01. Marched at 5 am to Blauwplatz (15 miles)**
**11-1-01. Marched at 5 am to Carnarvon. Made preparations to put the town in a state of defence.**
**12-1-01. Marched to Klipbankfontein (9 miles)**

*March, march, march, slog, slog, slog, boots, boots, boots... Roodidam, then Loesikop, then Goedfontein, then Fraserburg, that is 81 miles in 93 hours... if each pace is one yard, 1760 yards in a mile, that is over 140,000 paces in under four days... if we keep that up in seven days we will have marched a million paces... march, march, slog, slog... will my boots last? Will my feet last? Got to keep going, keep cheerful, set an example to the men... the men are wonderful, always moaning about the food, but never a grumble about the constant marching... we have to keep up the pace, the Boers are on the run... the new blockhouses look good, barbed wire round them and plenty of food and ammunition... . Colour Sergeant Fry's little set up at Sepani could hold out for ever... boots, boots, boots...*

**Digest of Service of 2nd Battalion Gloucestershire Regiment**

**10-2-01 . Marched to Wolvedams (22 miles)**
**11-2-01. Marched to Zand Hovel (14 miles)... Zand Balt (12 miles)... Deep Drift (9 miles)... Middleport (24 miles)... Matjesfontein (24 miles)... Toonplatz (25 miles)... Jackhalsfontein (9 miles)... Klipbankfontein (13 miles)... Longhouse (15 miles)... Aprils Kraal (18 miles)... Paalfontein (16 miles)... Matjesfontein (6 miles)**
**31-05-01. The Half Battalion left De Aar for Orange River Station, where it became part of Colonel Henry's column.**

**Part of a letter from Pte W Knight, 2nd Gloucester Regiment**

I was on the column commanded by Colonel Henry for 5 months and we did nearly 2,000 miles. We started at De Aar in the Cape Colony and went right through the Free State, and up into the Transvaal. We crossed the Vaal at Bloemhof and re-crossed going down again at Christiana and away down again into Cape Colony. Going up we passed Modder River, where the great battle took place, through Magersfontein, Klip Drift, Paardeberg, and we operated around Koffifontein, Christiana, Fourteen Streams, and Hoopstad.

Well, going up the country on the column we were banging away with the field guns and pom poms day after day. We had a few men killed but they belonged to the mounted infantry. We had our guns in action over 40 times. The Boers very nearly destroyed our column at the Vaal River. They set fire to the veldt, and it happened that the wind was blowing from behind, but it did not overtake us. We could hear the crackling of the flames and feel the heat.

We zig-zagged all over the shop from one place to another, and for the first three months we were continually marching, but for the last two months we had it much easier, for we stayed in one place for a few days while two or three portions of the column scoured the country. We caught about 600 Boer prisoners and brought in – I don't know how many women and children – both white and black, and while I think about it I must tell you that they are treated by our people as guests, and not as the papers and Campbell-Bannerman and Mrs Hobhouse state; in fact they get a better living than we poor Tommies do. They are put into camps and well looked after, all sorts of amusements are provided for them. The bands play for them and they get doctors, nurses and every comfort you can imagine. I saw where Mrs Hobhouse stated in the papers that she actually saw six living in one tent. What about us chaps? No tents at all; out in all sorts of weather for months at a time with only a couple of blankets.

# Chapter 1

**Digest of Service of 2nd Gloucestershire Regiment**

19-10-01. Entrained for Bloemfontein, which was reached on the following day, and joined the other half battalion, which had been holding a large portion of the defences.

22-10-01. E and F Companies under Lt Col Vines DSO left to garrison Sanna's Post.

21-2-02. D Company under Capt Whylock left to hold blockhouse line at Kroonstadt.

**The *Tewkesbury Mail* 29 January 1902**

We have been shown a letter from Private Knight, who is at Bloemfontein with the 2nd Gloucester Regiment.

'Dear Bill, I am thoroughly disgusted with Liberals, Radicals and such like politicians at home who believe in these false tales. I am on the spot, and have seen it with my own eyes. The lies which have been told is something disgraceful. Here are we chaps fighting and dying and always confronting disease and hardships, and there are so-called Englishmen at home telling the rottenest lies about us, about our cruelty and acts of brutality, and upholding the Boers, who have shot and wounded in cold blood, and murdered poor unarmed natives.

I think our people are too lenient with them. Lord Kitchener commutes half their sentences. I always thought he was a very severe man, but he is not half severe enough. Had it not been for the pro-Boers at home encouraging them I think the war would have been over long before this. If you have any pro-Boers in the dear old town of Tewkesbury, and should you come across them, be sure and don't do them any more harm than taking them down to the Swilgate or the Avon and holding their heads under water for about 10 minutes. They should be ashamed to call themselves English men the traitorous villains. It would be quite right if they were to hang every one of them for treason.

I forgot to tell you what sort of Christmas we had here. Last year it was bully beef and hard biscuits and a drink of water. This year we each had a small parcel. It contained a wooden pipe, a pair of socks, 1lb of tobacco, two plum puddings, box of matches, writing paper and envelope. We have a pint of beer here a day and it is appreciated. It goes down good.

I remain

Yours affectionately

W. Knight

*Bloemfontein*
*31 May 1902*

*Dear Mother*

*At last, it is all over! I have lost count of the hundreds and hundreds of miles I have marched, the dozens of pairs of boots I have worn out, but I do know exactly how many of my friends and comrades are no more, and how many have been grievously wounded. And all for a silly, stubborn old man, and his silly, stubborn followers. I know that the newspapers at Home are not always favourable to us, but I can reassure you that the Gloucestershire soldier is the gentlest, kindest, man you could meet – until he gets his dander up. And then you could not ask for a braver, more ardent comrade to join you in the fight.*

*I will not trouble you with my reflections on all the wickedness that we have seen on the part of the Boers. They are not all bad, and Tufnell and his men who were their prisoners for 17 days swore that they were well treated. But when I look at the ruin and despoliation that have come to this part of South Africa, it fair makes my blood boil. The Free Staters were not involved in the injustices meted out to the Uitlanders, but blindly followed Kruger, and brought all this misery down on themselves. I mention this, because we have come to know and rather like Bloemfontein, which is just as well because we have been told that we are to stay on here as garrison for some months or even years.*

*This brings me to the main purpose of this letter, which is to give you my thoughts on the future. I have, on the whole, enjoyed the*

# Chapter 1

*soldiering out here. Some parts have been beastly, but the spirit of the Regiment has been first class all the way through, and I want to stay with them. I had a long chat with Colonel Vines today, and he was kind enough to say some nice things about my conduct, most of all when I was commanding the company during Whylock's sickness. Any way, I am to be Assistant Adjutant next year, and attend the School of Musketry course as soon as we return to England. Chaps say that a lot of thinking will be done, and a lot of new ways are likely to be introduced. I intend to study hard and become a model soldier! Now, here's a go! You remember my House Master in Day Boys East, Dr Macgowan? I brought his son Oliver home to tea once. Any way, he is coming out to Grahamstown to be Headmaster of Saint Andrew's College, presumably as part of Milner's resettlement scheme. It is not too far down to the coast from here, so now that we can relax our vigilance against the Bittereinders, and the trains are running to full time table, I thought I might go down and look the old boy up. It would be good to get news of Cheltenham.*

*Finally, we are all to receive two medals for our service in the campaign – the Queen's medal, on which I shall have four clasps, and the King's medal, with two!*

*My love as always to the girls,*

*Yr affec son*
*Alexander*

**Extract from a Staff College lecture**

The Infantry Training Manual of 1902, which makes fascinating reading, is witness to the change in tactical thinking which was taking place. Its detailed instructions for long range rifle fire, its insistence on the use of cover, its concept of covering fire from rifles and machine guns, and its attention to individual initiative and to digging and trench construction, were revolutionary.

**Report from a foreign military observer, 1904**

In their manoeuvres the British infantry showed great skill in the use of ground. Their thin lines of khaki-clad skirmishers were scarcely visible. No detachment was ever seen in close order within three thousand yards. Frontal attacks were entirely avoided.

**Extract from the autobiography of Sir Edward Grey, Foreign Secretary**

Plans for naval and military cooperation with France had, I found, begun to be made under Lord Lansdowne in 1905, when the German pressure was menacing... But it was to be clearly understood that these conversations or plans between military or naval staffs did not commit either Government and involved no promise of support in time of war.

**Lord Haldane, appointed War Secretary in 1906, writes of Douglas Haig and Ellison, his collaborators in reforming the Army**

'The men one came across, the new school of young officers – entitled to the appellation of   men of science just as much as engineers or chemists – were to me a revelation... A new school of officers has arisen since the South African War, a thinking school of officers who desire to see the full efficiency which comes from new organisations and no surplus energy running to waste.'

# Chapter 1

**Lord Haldane, 1907**

'…..The National Army will, in future, consist of a Field Force and a Territorial or Home Force. The Field Force is to be so completely organised as to be ready in all respects for mobilisation immediately on the outbreak of a great war... The Territorial Force will be one of support and expansion, to be at once embodied when danger threatens, but not likely to be called for until after the expiration of the preliminary period of six months. It is hoped that men from the abolished militia will join the Special Reserve.'

(As a result the 3rd Battalion Gloucestershire Regiment (the old Royal South Gloucestershire Militia) becomes the 3rd (Special Reserve) Battalion the Gloucestershire Regiment. It is charged with training civilian volunteers to become individual reinforcements to the active Battalions).

**Part Two Orders, 2nd Battalion Gloucestershire Regiment, 12 July 1908**

**Capt Pagan, Assistant Adjutant, to be Adjutant, with immediate effect**

*Salamanca Barracks, Aldershot, home of 2nd Battalion, the Gloucestershire Regiment (61st Foot), 23 July 1909. At the Orderly Room the Commanding Officer is hearing Orders.*

*'Escort and Accused, quick march, leftrightleftrightmarktime...halt! Right turn! Private Williams, Sir.'*

*'Adjutant?'*

*'Sir, Private Williams is charged with drunkenness on duty, contrary to Section 21 of the Army Act 1881, in that he at Aldershot on 22 July 1909, while on a fatigue party, was drunk.'*

*'Williams, do you understand the nature of the charge?'*

*'Yes, Sir.'*

*'Do you wish to plead guilty or not guilty?'*

*'Guilty, Sir.'*

*'Evidence is from Lance Corporal Lilley.'*

'Sir, on 22 July I was in charge of a fatigue party clearing up the parade ground after the Salamanca Parade. I ordered Private Williams to pick up the marker flags, and I noticed that he was very slow to respond. I asked him if he had been drinking, and he stated that he had consumed a drop or two in the Regimental Institute after the parade. I thereupon placed him on the Report, Sir!'

'Private Williams?'

'After the parade, Sir, I took my rifle back to the arms kote, had a wet in the Institute , and was just sitting on my charpoy, sorting out my dhobi, when the Corporal comes in and says I'm needed for fatigue duty. He says to make it jildi but I was ally keefik so I said to imshi. He didn't like that, so I went with him to the parade ground. I admit, Sir, I was a bit slow with the flags.'

'Company Commander?'

'Sir, Williams is a senior soldier, with nineteen years service, much of it with the 28th in India and South Africa. He had a good chit from them when he came to us two years ago. He does his duties well in barracks and in the field, but he occasionally has too much beer. I think the fact that it was the Regimental Day caused him to celebrate unwisely. He has only two offences under this section in the last year, so you can deal with him summarily, Colonel. I would ask that you give him the benefit please Sir.'

'Very well, Williams, your Company Commander has spoken up for you, do you accept my award or do you wish to be tried by Court Martial?'

'Accept your award, Sir.'

'Very well, since it was Salamanca Day, I will be lenient. Seven days Confinement to Barracks.'

'Seven days CB, escort and accused, right turn, quickmarch, leftrightleftright...'

**From the *Daily Mail*, 28 March 1910**

When the Prince of Wales handed the Army Rugby Cup to Captain and Adjutant Pagan, Skipper of the 2nd Gloucesters at Twickenham on Saturday, one felt that the Gloucesters well deserved their victory. For 80 minutes both teams had played most strenuous football. The pace was tremendous, the tackling grim, and the character of the game the cleanest. The Gloucesters forwards were tougher and lasted better, and their defence was drastic.

No side at 80 minutes, so an extra 25 minutes each way. From a melee on the line, Corporal James, the tallest man on the field dived for a try. He was collared low and upended as he sprang, but as he landed on his head he managed to plant the ball on the line, and the Gloucesters won by this single try.

**Extract from a Staff College lecture**

The British Army's metamorphosis in the 10 years of the Edwardian era was as complete and far-reaching as anything achieved in the previous 100 or more. Field Service Regulations, promulgated in 1910, is a remarkable manual. Having established the necessity for coordination of all arms on the battlefield as a fundamental principle, the pamphlet addresses the tactical handling of machine guns, stressing the importance of surprise and protection from artillery fire of these crucial assets. It also pays great attention to night operations and trench warfare.

**Records of 3rd (Special Reserve) Battalion Gloucestershire Regiment**

**1-6-11. Capt Pagan reported from the 2nd Battalion for duty as Adjutant.**
**23-6-11. Annual Camp at Bulford, present 19 officers and 470 men.**
**1-7-11. Inspection by Lord Haldane, Secretary for War. The Times reported: 'The marching and movements in general were excellent... but in physique the men were far from equal to the Territorials.' We had a long wait during which a storm of rain came down. Lord Haldane was attired in an overcoat and top hat. His questions were far from illuminating, he actually thought the Permanent Staff (Second in Command, Adjutant, Quartermaster, etc) were S Reservists.**
**2-7-11. Lord Haldane did a tour of the camp lasting an hour. He asked the Commanding Officer a lot of questions – principally on the paucity of officers – but apparently had no solution to the question.**

# Gloucestershire Hero

*The marquee shudders in the night wind coming off Salisbury Plain. Storm lanterns sway and cast playful light and shadow on the officers in their scarlet mess jackets and blue patrols. The Mess Caterer anxiously shepherds his mixed staff, locally hired civilians and soldiers volunteering for the evening. He knows that the soldiers are supposed to be called Special Reservists, but to him they will always be militia.*

*The four courses are negotiated successfully, coffee is served, the port is circulated, the loyal toast and a toast for the Colonel-in-Chief are drunk. Cigars are passed and lit.*

*The guest of honour signals to those closest to him, among them the Commanding Officer and the Adjutant, to draw closer. He drops his voice.*

*'What I have to say is not for the newspapers. We have just heard that a German cruiser, the Panther, has moored off Agadir. They say that they are protecting German commercial interests, but the Government is not convinced of their motives. The Kaiser has been gearing up for a crisis for years – you all know how they are building up their Dreadnought fleet – but what a lot of people are not aware of is just how big their army is. They can put four million trained men in the field within a few weeks. It is no secret that I am a Germanophile – after all I went to one of their universities – but I am uneasy.*

*'This is where you chaps come in. I yield to none in my admiration for the British Army. The way it has buckled down to modernisation has been most praiseworthy, and I confess, an eye opener to me. But it is small! So small! Setting aside the overseas garrisons, and leaving a few thousand for Home Defence, we can put barely one hundred thousand regulars in the field. So you can see just how big a part you have to play. As soon as we take casualties, your officers and men will be taking their place. You have my wholehearted admiration for the way you do your duty as citizens and soldiers. Keep at it. England will need you.'*

# Chapter 1

**Records of 3rd (Special Reserve) Battalion the Gloucestershire Regiment**

20-6-12. Annual Camp at Porthcawl, present 18 officers and 450 men. The emphasis is to be on Battalion and Company training, shooting, defensive positions, digging trenches and night work.

10-7-12 Report on the Battalion rated musketry very satisfactory, machine gun training satisfactory.

## Letter from Foreign Secretary to HM the King, December 1912

Sir Edward Grey thinks it would be dangerous and misleading to let the German Government be under the impression that under no circumstances would England come to the assistance of France and Russia, if Germany and Austria went to war with them, and he thinks it very fortunate that Your Majesty was able to give an answer to Prince Henry that will prevent him from giving that impression to Berlin. Your Majesty's Government is not committed in the event of war and the public opinion of the country is, so far as Sir Edward Grey can judge, very adverse to a war arising out of a quarrel about Serbia. But if Austria attacked Serbia aggressively, and Germany attacked Russia if she came to the assistance of Serbia, and France were then involved, it might become necessary for England to fight for the defence of her position in Europe and for the protection of her own future and security.

**Records of 3rd (Special Service) Battalion the Gloucestershire Regiment**

23-6-13. Annual Camp at Felixstowe, present 17 officers and 486 men. The Inspecting Officer comments on 'A very satisfactory musketry efficiency'.

# Gloucestershire Hero

*Cheltenham*
*27 March 1914*

*My Dear Tommy*
*I cannot tell you how your letter astonished me! I will always remember our time at Sandhurst, you were our model for smartness and keenness. If anyone was going to get ahead it was you, and when you received the Cavalry Medal, we all thought it was the seal on a successful eighteen months, and the start of something really big with the Donkey Wallopers. Now your news has absolutely bowled me over.*

*You do not say exactly what has caused your decision, and I picked up a hint that you may not be the only one. Is it all to do with the unrest in the North? I know the Ulster Volunteers are making a big show, and of course we are all sympathetic to their desire to remain in the Union, but surely all this drilling and speechifying is just a show? Of course we do not have the first hand knowledge that you have being so close to Dublin, and I am glad you have put me in the picture on one or two things. But Tommy old boy! To throw away your career! We need chaps like you – who is going to put me on his horse and take me to safety when the Germans shoot me if you are not there!*

*However it all turns out, I know you will do the right thing, and I wish you all the luck in the world in the next few weeks.*

*Your affectionate chum*
*Patsy*

**Records of 3rd (Special Service) Battalion the Gloucestershire Regiment**

**20-6-14. Annual Camp at Perham Down, present 20 officers and 503 men.**

# Chapter 1

28 June 1914.   Serbian irredentists assassinate Archduke Franz-Ferdinand of Austria-Hungary.

23 July 1914.   Austria-Hungary sends an ultimatum to Serbia containing several very severe demands, demanding compliance within forty-eight hours.

24 July 1914.   Germany declares support for Austria-Hungary's position.

25 July 1914.   Serbia agrees to most of Austria-Hungary's demands, and requests that the Hague Tribunal arbitrate on those matters which put in question her survival as a nation. Russia enters a period preparatory to war. Serbia mobilizes.

28 July 1914.   Austria-Hungary declares war on Serbia.

29 July 1914.   Germany, contemplating war with France, seeks Britain's neutrality if German forces violate Belgium's neutrality.

1 August 1914.   French mobilization is ordered, German mobilization is ordered, and Germany declares war against Russia.

3 August 1914.   Germany declares war on France.

'The lights are going out all over Europe. We shall not see them lit again in our lifetime.'
   Sir Edward Grey, Foreign Secretary

Records of 3rd (Special Service) Battalion the Gloucestershire regiment.

4-8-14. Orders received to mobilize.
8-8-14. Battalion called up. 22 officers and 550 men report for duty Detachments to Abbey Wood and Plumstead Marshes.
11-8-14. Adjutant's parade.
15-8-14. Suspect German caught in the river near the Sewage Works.
12-9-14. A reservist up at Orderly Room for resisting the police and drunk in town gives the following excuse: 'The remarks of a 'lady' outside a public house were not complimentary to the Regiment and excited his anger.'

Part Two Orders, 3rd (Special Service) Battalion the Gloucestershire Regiment, 3 January 1915

<u>Postings and Movements</u>
Capt Pagan relinquishes the post of Adjutant, and is posted to 1st Battalion, BEF, France

# Chapter 2

War Diary, 1915, 1st Battalion the Gloucestershire Regiment, (28th), Givenchy, France

**15th Jan.** Situation unchanged, quiet day. A Coy relieved at 6.30 am by R. Munster Fus and withdrawn to reserve, just south of PONT FIXE.
Capt A W Pagan, 3rd Battn (R.E.) and 2 Lt Bennett, King's Own S R joined.
1 killed, 1 wounded.

By 15 January 1915, the Battalion is largely composed of 'National Reservists', who have long since finished their service in the reserve; many of them had left the colours before the South African War. They received no retaining fee, but contracted to serve on mobilisation in return for a prospective payment of £10. They are elderly gentlemen; they are not mobile; but they bear the brunt of winter in the crudely fashioned trenches. They make tea and fry bacon by day or by night in rain and frost and snow, without dugouts or shelters, and up to their knees in horrible slush. Only four officers now remain who have served continuously with the 28th since the war began. The companies, whose average strength is ninety men, have in their ranks few who landed in France with the regiment, and most of the surplus reservists and the men of the 3rd Battalion, sent out as reinforcements, have also disappeared, while hardly any of those who enlisted at the outbreak of war have yet reached France.

The line lies just east of the village of Givenchy and consists of a narrow ditch, deep in mud and water; there are no support or communication trenches. The only revetting materials available are a few sandbags, so shift is made with the doors of houses, iron bedsteads and the like, to stop the trenches collapsing completely. Sleep is impossible, an uneasy doze the only escape. Fortunately, braziers, firewood and food are abundant. In places the German lines are less than 100 yards away.

Battalion headquarters is in a house on the south bank of the Aire La Bassée Canal, close to an iron bridge called Pont Fixe, smashed by shell fire, but passable on foot. The line is held by two companies, with one in battalion reserve, and one in brigade reserve. The reserve companies are lodged in Harley Street, a road leading from the Bethune-La Bassée road to Pont Fixe. The houses are comfortable enough, but are sprayed with bullets day and night, which detracts from the ease of the resting troops.

War Diary, 1915, 1st Battalion the Gloucestershire Regiment, (28th), Givenchy

25th Jan. At 6.45 am hostile artillery commenced heavy bombardment, and many bombs were thrown at our trenches. Except in one portion of our trench, which was completely destroyed, little damage was done.

At 7.30 am a rocket was sent up, which apparently was the signal for the infantry to attack. We were able to bring effective fire to bear on them, causing many of them to retire to their trenches, but large numbers still came on, being eventually brought to a standstill 40 to 50 yards from our trenches. At this time, Capt Richmond and Capt George were killed, and one of the machine guns was put out of action. 2Lt Hodges, now in command of D Coy, sent reinforcements to our left trench, to face both front and rear, as the enemy were now in the village. C Company, in Bde reserve at LE PREOL, had 1 officer and 4 men killed, 1 officer and 3 men wounded on their way up to PONT FIXE.

Capt Pagan to command C Company, vice Capt Foord, wounded.

# Chapter 2

France
23rd February 1915

Dear Mother

We have moved to a new area, where we are able to rest and train. The surroundings are pleasant enough, despite many slag heaps and mine buildings. The undulating countryside is dotted with small coverts, and nearby is a magnificent forest, untouched by the war.

The billets we first occupied were draughty and uncomfortable, but by degrees most of the men were lodged in private houses. The village consists almost entirely of miners' cottages with a few farms on the outskirts. Once extricated from the dilapidated barns of the farms, from the lofts of the village school, and from the goods yard of the local station, and put into cottages, the men became quite comfortable. Once the fashion of putting up soldiers in their houses had been established among the inhabitants the demand did not equal the supply and many children were bitterly disappointed by the refusal of their requests for 'Cinq ou six soldats'.

The people are very friendly, and get on well with the men – Gloucestershire men always get on well with everyone – and look after them. Some even get their boots cleaned in the morning!

Sadly, we soon say goodbye to the Colonel, he will be sadly missed. I have had a letter from Foord, who you will remember did so well with the 61st in South Africa. He is recovering slowly in hospital in England, perhaps you might be able to visit him. You will also want to know about Corporal James, the giant who you will remember scored the winning try in the Army Cup final in 1910. He was recalled from the Reserve in 1914, rapidly rose to Company Sergeant Major and was sadly killed last December. I am pleased to say that we have found his grave in the village, and been able to smarten it up.

The weather continues wet and cold with a good deal of snow and frost, but there is an occasional feeling of spring in the air, and the birds are beginning to sing.

Your affectionate son
Alexander

On 14 March, the 28th, with the rest of 3 Brigade, moves into divisional reserve, and marches to Hinges, a pretty village on a hill, very English in appearance, with its fields, trees and hedgerows. The hill is only 130 feet above sea level, but, compared with the flat plain that surrounds it, appears to be a mountain. The weather is warm and spring-like. The hawthorn hedges are getting green; the earth is drying; the men get baths and clean clothes.

Mild training and route marching are carried out, a boxing tournament is held, and football is played. The rest period ends on 22 March, when the Battalion returns to the line.

**War Diary, 1915, 1st Battalion the Gloucestershire Regiment (28th)**

**23rd March. Some shelling, but no serious damage. In the evening the battn relieved R Berks R in trenches at NEUVE CHAPELLE. Relief completed by 8.30 pm.**

**24th March. Situation remains unchanged. Hostile snipers very active from the NW corner of BOIS DE BIEZ, and slight shelling by the enemy, mostly falling near BREWERY to the rear of our right trench. Our companies were very energetic in counter sniping. Capt Pagan slightly wounded in arm.**

**25th March. Situation remains unchanged, all quiet. Mr PALMER, American war correspondent withthe British Army, spent the night in the trenches, and returned to GHQ next morning.**

**From the report of Mr Palmer:**

Around us was utter silence, where the hell of thunders and destruction by the artillery had raged during the battle. Then a spent or ricochet bullet swept overhead, with the whistle of complaint of spent bullets at having travelled far without hitting any object. It had gone high over the British trenches; it had carried the full range, and the chance of it hitting anything was ridiculously small. But the nearer you get to the trenches, the more likely these strays are to find a victim.

At last we felt the solidity of a paved road under our feet, and following this we came to a peasant's cottage. Inside two soldiers were sitting beside telephone and telegraph instruments, behind a window stuffed with sandbags. On our way across the fields we had stepped on wires laid on the ground; we had stooped to avoid wires stretched on poles – the wires that form the web of the army's intelligence. Of course there is always a duplicate, so if one is broken it is immediately repaired.

These two men at the table, their faces tanned by exposure, men in the thirties, had the British regular of long service stamped all over them. War was an old story to them, and an old story, too, laying signal wires under fire.

'We're very comfortable,' said one, 'No danger from stray bullets or shrapnel; but if one of the Jack Johnsons comes in, why, there's no more cottage and no more argument between you and me. We're dead and maybe buried, or maybe scattered over the landscape, along with the broken pieces of the roof.'

I stooped to feel my way down three or four narrow steps to the cellar, where there were straw beds around the walls. The major commanding the Battalion rose from his seat at a table on which there was some cutlery, a jam pot, tobacco, pipes, a newspaper or two, and army telegraph forms and maps. He introduced me to an officer sitting on the other side of the table and to one lying in his blankets against the wall, who lifted his head and blinked and said he was very glad to see me.

'How is it? Painful now?' asked the major of Captain Pagan, on the other side of the table.

'Oh, no, it's quite all right,' he replied.

'Using the sling?'

'Part of the time. Hardly need it though.'

Captain Pagan was one of those men whose eyes are always smiling; who seems, wherever he is, to be glad that he is not in a worse place; who goes right on smiling at the mud in the trenches and bullets and shells and death. They are not emotional, the British, perhaps, but they are given to cheeriness, if not to laughter, and they have a way of smiling at times when smiles are much needed. The smile is more often found at the front than back at headquarters; or perhaps it is more noticeable there.

'You see, he got a bullet through the arm yesterday,' the major explained.' He was reported wounded, but remained on duty in the trench.' I saw that Captain Pagan would rather not have publicity given to such an ordinary incident. He did not see why people should talk about his arm. 'You are to go with him into the trench for the night,' the major added; and I thought myself very lucky in my companion.

'Aren't you going to have dinner with us?' the major asked him.

'Why I had something to eat not very long ago,' said Captain Pagan. One was not sure whether he had or not.

'There's plenty,' said the major.

'In that event I don't see why I shouldn't eat when I have a chance,' the captain returned; which I found was a characteristic trench habit, particularly in winter when exposure to the raw, cold air calls for plenty of body-furnace heat.

We had ration soup and ration ham and ration prunes and cheese: what Tommy Atkins gets. When we were outside the house and starting for the trench, the captain, with his wounded arm, wanted to carry my knapsack.

Where we turned off the road, broken finger-points of brick walls in the faint moonlight indicated the site of Neuve Chapelle; other fragments of wall in front of us were the remains of a house; and that broken tree-trunk showed what a big shell can do. All this had been in the field of that battle which was as fierce as Gettysburg. Every tree, every square yard of ground, had been paid for by shells, bullets and human life. Now we were near the trenches; or, rather the breastworks. Not all parts of the line are held by trenches. A trench is dug in the ground, a breastwork is raised from the level of the ground.

We came into the open and heard the sound of voices and saw a spotty white wall; for some of the sandbags of the new British breastworks still retained their original colour. On the reverse side of the wall rifles were waiting in readiness, their fixed bayonets faintly gleaming in the moonlight. I felt the edge of one and it was sharp, quite prepared for business. In the surroundings of damp earth and mud-bespattered men, this rifle seemed the cleanest thing of all, meticulously clean, that ready weapon whose well-aimed and telling fire, in obedient and cool hands, was the object of all the drill of the infantry of England.

Across a reach of field faintly were made out the white spots of another wall of breastworks, the German, at the edge of the Bois de Biez. The British reached these woods in their advance; but, their aeroplanes being unable to spot the fall of shells in the mist, they had to fall back for want of artillery support. Along this line the defence with rifles and machine guns had riddled the German counter-attack.

'Now, which is my house?' asked Captain Pagan.

'I really can't find my own house in the dark.'

Asking me to wait until he made a light the captain bent over as if to crawl under the top rail of a fence and his head disappeared. After he had put a match to a candle and stuck it onto a stick thrust into the wall, I could see the interior of this habitation. A rubber sheet spread on the moist earth served as floor, carpet, mattress and bed. At a squeeze there was room for two others beside myself.

'Quite cosy, don't you think?' remarked the captain. But then, he was the kind of man who might sleep in a muddy field under a wagon, and regard that as luxury. 'Leave your knapsack here,' he continued, and we'll see what is doing along the line.'

'Not quite so loud,' he warned a soldier who was bringing up boards from the rear under cover of darkness. 'If the Germans hear they may start firing.'

Two other men were piling mud on top of a section of breastwork at an angle to the mainline. 'What is that for?'

'They got an enfilade on us here, Sir, and we wanted to make it higher.'

'That's no good. A bullet will go right through that. We'll have to wait until we have more sandbags.'

A little further on half a dozen men were piling earth to extend the breastwork.

'How does it go?' asks Captain Pagan.

'Very well, Sir, though what we need is sandbags.'

'We'll have some up tomorrow.'

A deep, broad ditch filled with water made a break in our line.

'A little bridging is required here,' said the captain. 'We'll have it done tomorrow night. The break is no disadvantage if they attack; in fact we'd rather have them make a try for it. But it makes movement along the line by day difficult.'

When we were across, he called my attention to some high ground in the rear.

'One of our officers took a short cut across there in daylight,' he said. 'He was quite exposed and they got him through the arm. It wasn't cricket for anyone to go out and bring him in, but he managed to crawl to cover.'

Values are relative, and a brazier in the trenches makes for comfort. You are at home there with Tommy Atkins, regular of an old line English regiment, in his heavy khaki overcoat and solid boots and wool puttees, a sturdy, hardened man of a terrific war. He, the regular, the shilling-a-day policeman of the empire, was still doing the fighting at the front. This man and that one were at Mons. This one and that one had been through the whole campaign without once seeing Mother England for which they were fighting.

The affection in which Captain Pagan was held extended throughout the regiment, for we had left his own company behind. At every turn he was asked about his arm. Oh but the captain was bored with hearing about that arm! If he is wounded again I am sure that he will try to keep the fact a secret.

These veterans could 'grouse' as the British call it. Grousing is one of Tommy's privileges. Their language was yours, the language in which our own laws and schoolbooks are written. I asked if they ever had any doubt that they would reach the Rhine.

'How could we, Sir!'

Believing in the old remedy for exhaustion and exposure to cold, the army served out a tot of rum every day to the men. But many of them are teetotallers, these hardy regulars, so they asked for chocolate instead.

As we proceeded on our way, officers came out of the little houses to meet Captain Pagan and the strange American civilian.

'How are things going on over your side?'

'Nicely.'

'Any shelling?'

'A little this morning, no harm done.'

'We cleaned out one bad sniper today.'

'Ought to have some sandbags up tonight.'

Just then a couple of bullets went singing overhead. The group paid no attention. It was time that Captain Pagan was back to his own command. As we came to his company's line word was just being passed from sentry to sentry 'No firing, patrols going out.'

'We'll go in the other direction' said Captain Pagan.

By mid-April there are present with the Battalion thirty four NCOs and eighty-two men who have served continuously during the campaign. On the 22nd, the 28th goes into reserve about Le Touret and Richebourg St Vaast. This village is little damaged, but uninhabited, with huge shell holes in the churchyard. On the 24th, the Battalion returns to Hinges for ten days. The weather is balmy, and nightingales, under a red moon set in a cloudless sky, practise their uncertain song all night. The fields, with their elms, whose boughs show dark through a mist of the clearest green, their hedges and their bright spring grass, remind one of England. A great chestnut, shading a road junction near Le Vertannoy, is in full leaf.

In early May, the stage is set for the battle of the Aubers Ridge.

**War Diary, 1915, 1st Battalion the Gloucestershire Regiment (28th)**

**5th May. Training in wood fighting by companies in BOIS DE PACAULT CO and Capt Pagan attended conference at Brigade HQ.
Capt Pagan assumed command of the Battalion from today's date.**

The attack on the Aubers Ridge is to be carried out by the First British Army, in which the 28th are in 3 Brigade of the 1st Division of I Corps. They are a small fragment of the many thousands whose task is to attack from just south of Neuve Chapelle and from west of Fromelles.

The plan for 3 Brigade is to attack from Richebourg l'Avoué. The bombardment is to become intense at 0530 on 8 May, and at 0540 the 2nd Royal Munster Fusiliers and the 2nd Welch are to capture the first line of German trenches. At the same time, the 1st Gloucesters and 1st South Wales Borderers are to move forward to the British front line, there to await the order to advance. They are then to advance through the assaulting battalions to further objectives.

On 6 May, Captain Pagan, acting commanding officer, takes his company commanders forward to reconnoitre the ground over which the attack will take place. At 1900 on 7 May, the Battalion is assembled to march forward, when news is received that the attack is to be delayed. On the evening of 8 May, the 800 men who are due to attack move off. They march through deserted villages, where only the howling of dogs greets them, for the eleven miles to their assembly position; there they spend the night in drawing bombs, respirators, rations and other stores.

It is a delightfully fresh spring morning, with a cloudless sky, when the Munsters and the Welch climb out of their trenches to be greeted by a storm of machine gun and rifle fire. Some of the Munsters, led by their commanding officer, disappear into the enemy's trenches; but the attack, crumbling under a hail of bullets, comes to a standstill. The Gloucesters, following up, find the trenches which should be their 'jumping off point' crammed with men.

Communication is almost impossible within this jumbled mass, but the 28th somehow sort themselves so that C Company is on the right, B on the left, and D in Support. At 0700 they renew the attack, those without orders following their comrades when they see them leave the safety of the front line to move forward. The attempt, met immediately by overwhelming machine gun fire, dies out after fifty yards are covered at huge cost. Eventually, orders are given for the survivors to return to our line, and then back to our third-line trenches.

At 1100 the 28th are ordered to repeat the attack in the afternoon. By now the front line trenches are less congested, and the regiment assembles with D Company on the right, A on the left, and B and C in support. D Company, gallantly led by Captain Brodigan, gets forward over 100 yards, but loses all of its officers, most of its NCOs and ninety men. As darkness falls, the wounded are brought in. The total casualties are eleven officers and 253 other ranks.

# Chapter 2

Battalion Headquarters
1st Battalion the
Gloucestershire Regiment
Headquarters
3rd Infantry Brigade

## Battle of the Aubers Ridge

The success gained in the early stages of the Neuve Chapelle battle encouraged the belief that the German line could be broken with the same tactics and with the same expenditure of ammunition. But the enemy, having learned his lesson, was not to be caught napping again. His positions were enormously strengthened from the beginning of March; the attack, this time, was not a surprise to him.

The power of our artillery was nothing like sufficient to overcome his small-arms fire, and directly our troops crossed their parapets he was up and at them; our barrages did not deter him in the least. There was no covering rifle or machine-gun fire on our part, no attempt to progress by fire and movement, and once the artillery bombardment had failed, in these lay the only chance of success.

This was partly due to lack of training, and partly due to the fact that we had to cross a parapet, then to be immediately at close quarters with a foe who had no flank, but to whose flanking and enfilade fire we were continually exposed.

It is recommended that new methods be adopted to overcome these difficulties.

A W Pagan
Captain
A/Commanding Officer

# Gloucestershire Hero

France
16th May 1915

Dear Mother

*We have had a pretty difficult time since I last wrote, and I am sorry to say that we have lost some very fine officers and men. I commanded the Battalion in the recent action, during Gardiner's absence, and I was much heartened by the way that everyone behaved. I cannot give you details, but one thing I can say is that the agitation in the Daily Mail for an adequate supply of artillery ammunition is not before time, and much welcomed. I was sorry to see that Northcliffe was heaped with abuse in some quarters, but I can tell you we are right behind him.*

*My present headquarters is in a charming little underground, two-roomed cottage with a roof of curved iron. In front, opening on to the trenches, is a partially roofed veranda, with seats on three sides, from which steps lead down into the house; the whole is painted pale blue. The walls and roof of the living room are papered, and everywhere are polished shell cases full of lilac. It is called 'Villa Beau Terrier'.*

*The nearby Chateau has a delightful garden. It is rumoured that its owner, a very old man, is still there, though he is never seen. He keeps pigs, and has a large aviary. I am also pleased to tell you that local prices are low, and the men have had baths and a much needed change of clothing. There will be one or two coming on leave to Cheltenham soon, they may look you up and bring you more news which I cannot include here. I am quite well, and feel very fit.*

*Your very affec son*
*Alexander*

**War Diary (1915) of 1st Battalion the Gloucestershire Regiment (28th)**

**29th May. Maj Gardiner returns from base and assumes command. Capt Pagan reverts to command of C Company.**

Slowly the 28th lick their wounds; replacements for their heavy losses arrive and are quickly welcomed and knitted into the tight structure of the regiment. A quiet sector is occupied, the enemy's trenches are some way off, and only the incessant rumble of transport on the pavé roads disturbs the even tenor of life.

In June, life improves even more when the 28th are withdrawn to Bethune. The surroundings here are delightful, particularly in the neighbourhood of the railway embankment south of the church. The fields are full of long grass and the seedlings from last year's crops; everywhere are patches of scarlet poppies and vivid blue cornflowers. The days pass pleasantly and idly in perfect weather; by night working parties go up the line to dig trenches.

The men are quartered in the tobacco factory, where they are comfortably settled. Baths are available, as is fresh clothing; for some undiscovered reason, blankets have to be handed in.

Bethune is a large town with plenty of shops and estaminets; most of the inhabitants remain, and the shops and markets do excellent business. All sorts of supplies are obtainable, excellent fish can be bought daily, and the banks are open for business. Frequent concerts are held in the French theatre, a Brigade boxing meeting takes place, as do swimming sports and athletics. Best of all, leave is granted to those NCOs and men who have been in France since the beginning of the war.

*France*
*25th June*

*Dear Mother*
*I am happy to tell you that we are still enjoying restful days. We have moved again, but the new village is very pleasant. Eggs, milk, green peas and strawberries are plentiful, good, and cheap. We are all billeted in large farms and houses, and the people are very friendly.*
*One problem which is becoming ever more pressing is the age of some of our reservists. They can do their work in the line, even digging,*

*but they cannot march, and battalion moves are accomplished only by resorting to desperate measures, such as hiring carts.*

*I am sorry to say that there is one item which disturbs our otherwise gentle existence, and that is the news from home. Definite reports – on top of the rumours that have been with us for some time – are beginning to reach us of strikes and refusals to go all out with their work on the part of some of those engaged in England at employment essential to the war. We regular soldiers are only doing in France what we are paid for – it is part of our profession. We have neither the right nor the wish to resent the behaviour of these ill-humoured workers. But for the increasing number of those among us who hastened to join at the outset of war, such conduct appears odd, and is the subject of considerable discussion.*

*My fondest love to the girls, I remain*

*Your very affectionate*
*Alexander*

On 19 July the 28th take over the sector known as 'Bomb Alley,' a repulsive place where day and night the enemy hurl at them a great variety of mortar shells and rifle grenades. This is very tiring to all, and hair-raising experiences abound. On 25 July an officer on trench duty is standing near a sentry, one newly joined and unaccustomed to the turmoil of the line. A rifle grenade appears in the sky, descending directly on the sentry, who is so interested that he makes no move. The officer thrusts him into the mouth of a dugout just in time. Later, he is with a corporal when they see another bomb above him, twirling slowly down. They lie flat and the bomb explodes on the parados a foot above their heads. They are extricated, nervous but unharmed, from the earth and wreckage which cover them.

# Chapter 2

**War Diary (1915) of 1st Battalion the Gloucestershire Regiment (28th)**

26th July. Resting
27th July. Training
28th July. Training, Capt Pagan confirmed in command of the Battalion in the acting rank of Lt Col.
29th July. Training.
30th.July. 3rd Bde horse show at ANNEZIN.

On 4 August the 28th take over a quiet sector. Shelling is infrequent, the lines are too far apart for rifle fire, and life is placid and pleasant. The weather is warm, and the trenches are really excellent. The science of trench maintenance has improved enormously, and every one is well drained and well revetted; the traverses are wide and solid, and the floors are boarded and even. These advantages, aided by the dry weather, make it possible to keep the trenches scrupulously clean; they are swept morning and evening. The general standard of living is higher than ever.

However, a feeling is abroad that big things are imminent. The soldier feels a gentle melancholy at the approach of a big battle; not because he feels their result as regards himself, but because he knows that he is likely to lose many with whom he has served in great good fellowship.

On 7 September, the Commander of the 1st Division is promoted, and replaced by Major General Holland. He makes a good initial impression by appearing from No Man's Land and climbing into the front line trench.

As the month progresses, so do the preparations for the great battle. Gas cylinders have to be carried up from their dumps near Versselles to their emplacements in the front line. The work is extremely hard because the cylinders are heavy and unwieldy, and the communication trenches along which they have to be borne are long and twisty.

Commanding officers are taken forward to view the ground over which the attack will take place. Orders are distributed for the Battle of Loos.

OPERATION ORDER No. 38

## BY BRIGADIER GENERAL H R DAVIES
## COMMANDING 3rd INFANTRY BRIGADE

### 22nd SEPTEMBER 1915

The 1st Army is assuming the offensive on the morning of the ** instant, and the 4th Corps has been ordered to attack the enemy's positions between the DOUBLE CRASSIER and the VERSELLES–HULLUCH Road. Simultaneously strong attacks will be delivered by the French on the South and the 1st Corps on the North.

The 1st Division will attack on the front Northern Sap inclusive – the HULLUCH Road exclusive. The 1st and 2nd Infantry Brigades will carry out the assault. The 3rd Infantry Brigade will be in Divisional Reserve. GREEN'S Force will establish itself in the front line of enemy trenches as soon as they have been cleared. Its mission thereafter is to watch for, and move forward to meet, any counter-attack which the enemy may attempt to push in between the 1st and 2nd Infantry Brigades.

Immediately prior to the assault, gas alternating with smoke will be discharged from the front trenches along the whole front. This will be carried out under the direction of OC 187th Company R.E., and will be extended over a period of 40 (forty) minutes. The discharge will be at once followed by the assault. This will take place at a fixed time and will be communicated to all concerned.

The 3rd Brigade will move into its position of readiness on the night of 24th/25th September, as follows:

1st Bn Gloucestershire Regiment at 1.0 am from 'D' Area to TRENCH 16.A, STROUD ROAD, BRISTOL ROAD, CHELTENHAM ROAD, TEWKESBURY ROAD, USK ROAD, as far north as junction with CLIFTON ROAD exclusive..........

# Chapter 2

It is very important that while in these positions there should be no movement that would show to the enemy. Bayonets must not be fixed, and no rifles or flags must show above the parapet. No fires must be lit. In all movement along trenches, care must be taken that rifles and flags do not show.

As the 1st and 2nd Infantry Brigades and GREEN'S Force advance, the 3rd Infantry Brigade will occupy the trenches they vacate as follows:
1st Bn the Gloucestershire Regiment. First the Old Fire and Support Trenches, and subsequently, when they are vacated, from 'A'2 to near 'B'2, by point 'A'.

A bomb carrying party will be organised by each battalion, consisting of one officer or NCO and 10 men, whose duty it will be to carry bombs forward from the bomb stores so as to ensure that the bomb throwers in front have enough.

Each man will carry:
> Rations for the 25th beside the iron ration
> Filled water bottle
> 2 Sandbags
> 2 Smoke Helmets
> Waterproof Sheet
> 220 rounds of ammunition

Bombers will carry 5 cricket ball bombs each in bomb bandoliers. The bombs will be drawn from the bomb-fusing house in VERQUIN.

Flags will be carried as follows: a red flag, 2' x 2' with vertical white stripes, by 4 men per platoon. A similar flag, 1' x 1' on a 5ft pole, to be carried by one man per bombing squad. A black screen with white diagonal stripes on a 3ft pole to be carried by the bomb supply party to be planted in the German trenches to show the position of bomb stores.

Every effort will be made to rest men as much as possible on the 24th, and all issuing and other arrangements should be done in daytime, so that all ranks can sleep in the early part of the night. Tea should be arranged before starting on the night march. Cookers will follow battalions on the march and will draw out at CORON DE RUTOIRE, so that a tea meal can be brought up from there to the trenches for breakfast on the 25th. Tea meal will be sent up as soon as possible after the battalions have got into their positions and the cookers will start back for the 1st Line Transport not later than 7.0 am.

Stores of S.A.A, Verey light ammunition and bombs have been established along the Old Support Trench. These are for use by the 3rd Brigade, and are marked by placards.

On arrival in the position of readiness, each battalion will send 8 men to Brigade Headquarters at LE RUTOIRE FARM to draw two Vermorel anti-gas sprayers and eight tins of solution per battalion.

Orderlies carrying messages between Brigade Headquarters and Battalions will wear a blue and white armband. Any man wearing this armband who becomes a casualty should be searched for the message which ought to be in the right breast pocket, and the message should be forwarded to its destination. A system of runners at the rate of 3 per Battalion Headquarters and 4 per company should be arranged to supplement other means of communication.

There is no danger in following up the gas in the open, but no one should enter a German trench, dug-out or cellar, without having his smoke helmet properly fastened, as the gas sinks into these and remains there until dispersed by the Vermorel sprayer. No food or water found in German trenches should be used as it will be poisoned by the gas. Five shelters have been established by the 1st and 2nd Brigades as Regimental Aid Posts behind the old Support Trenches. These will be available to the 3rd Brigade when they occupy these trenches.

Prisoners will be sent under escort to LE RUTOIRE FARM, where they will be handed over to an escort provided by the A.P.M.

C.N.Berkeley
Brigade Major

# Chapter 2

Battalion Operation Order by Lt Col A W Pagan, Commanding 1st Gloucesters

The Battn will move into a position of readiness as follows:
A Coy, move by FRENCH ALLEY – CLIFTON RD – USK RD into that portion of Trench 16A between USK RD and STROUD RD.
B Coy move by FRENCH ALLEY – CLIFTON RD into CHELTENHAM RD and BRISTOL RD as far as STROUD RD.
C Coy move by FRENCH ALLEY – CLIFTON RD into that portion of USK RD between TRENCH 16A and CLIFTON RD and into TEWKESBURY RD.
D Coy move by FRENCH ALLEY – SEVERN RD, turn west into USK RD past BURNT RICKS by BARRY RD into that portion of BARRY RD between BURNT RICKS and junction of USK RD and TRENCH 16A.

As Battns of 1st and 2nd Brigades vacate our own trenches, the Battalion will move as follows:

A Coy moves by Trench 16A past point A by BOYAU A.I. into old FIRE TRENCH along OLD FIRE TRENCH to board marked 'Right of 1st Brigade' between BOYAU B1 and B2. A Coy will be left front line coy from this point.

B Coy moves...
When NEW SUPPORT and FIRE TRENCHES have been vacated by 1st and 2nd Bdes, Coys will move as follows:
A Coy by SAP B1 into new FIRE TRENCH left resting on board marked 'Right of 1st Bde'.
B Coy by SAP B...

Machine Gun Section, during all moves after arriving at FRENCH TRENCHES, 2 guns will move in front of or on left of C Coy, 2 guns will move in rear or right of D Coy. 1 Lewis Gun will move in front of or on left of D Coy.

In all movements, Coy Commanders will move at the head of their coys, and while in FRENCH TRENCHES will be at that end of their Coys nearest to route to Point A.

Bn Hdqtrs. Position of C.O. will be as follows: in FRENCH TRENCHES, at junction of STROUD RD and TRENCH 16A. In NEW SUPPORT LINE at Junction of NEW SUPPORT LINE with BOYAU B. When Front Line Coys leave our new FIRE TRENCH, C.O. will move in centre of FRONT LINE.

The attack is launched at 0630, on 25 September, preceded by a discharge of gas along the whole British front south of the canal. From its position in reserve, the 28th have an excellent view of the advance of the divisions to the south, and the watchers are thrilled by the rapidity, good style and apparent ease with which our troops go forward.

The attack by the 1st Division, however, is not nearly so successful. Two Brigade is completely held up and never penetrates the enemy front line. The failure is mainly due to the gas being blown back into our trenches, but also to the very gallant defence put up by the Germans in that sector. One Brigade on its left is more successful, and captures the enemy's front and support lines. Green's force is ordered to attack where 2 Brigade has failed, and the 28th is ordered to move forward into the front line trenches.

Green's force, lacking the support of the artillery which has moved on to further objectives, makes a gallant attempt, but fails, and hampers the forward movement of the 28th. At 1415 an order is received from 1st Division.

**From: 1 Div    To: 2nd Bde    PRIORITY**

First Gloucesters are placed at your disposal aaa. Collect all available men of your own brigade subject to leaving sufficient to hold your own line aaa Move these men together with first gloucesters down past RED FLAG to LOOS road and cross into German trench at the northern LOOS salient aaa Then wheel up to your left and attack along line of NORTH LOOS AVENUE and metalled LOOS-LA BASSÉE road so as to get behind Germans holding up your brigade aaa 15th Div inform me that one of their battalions is hung up opposite southern sap and when your advance across

# Chapter 2

to Northern LOOS salient takes place you will be able to take this 15th Div battalion along with you. Copied to 3rd Bde who should understand that first gloucesters are no longer at their disposal.

**Adv 1st Div**

The Regiment moves off at once with a view to gaining a position to outflank the defenders. Just as it begins to deploy, however, 400 of the enemy surrender, and the position is taken. The Commander of 2 Brigade now orders the 28th to occupy the Bois Hugo, two miles from the front line. The Regiment shakes out into open formation, and begins to move south west, unhindered by the Germans.

*It is exciting, this advance over coarse autumn grass on land that was so recently, and for so long, occupied by the enemy. Rifle fire from buildings half a mile way interrupts this peaceful progress, but by skilful use of ground the Bois Hugo is reached with little loss, company positions are allotted, and the men begin to dig in. As dusk approaches the Regiment is joined by the remnants of the 2nd Brigade.*

*It is now that leadership is tested. The men are very tired, those of the 2nd Brigade have seen many of their number blown to pieces, the ground is hard for digging. He cannot rest, and he is everywhere; here, directing the siting of a trench, there, the clearance of a field of fire. He takes particular care over the siting of his machine-guns. He addresses every man by name, encouraging, cajoling, occasionally reprimanding. So the weary scraping in the solid chalk continues for hour after hour throughout the night.*

*The Germans counter-attack – at first, light probing attacks, then with the dawn, they come on with more determination. They are easily beaten off, but casualties mount.*

*The Adjutant, Captain Bosanquet, has a miraculous escape. As he oversees the digging he suddenly falls flat on his face, and two bullet holes are found in his jacket on each side of his backbone. Amazingly, he recovers after a few minutes, and the bullet is found to have grazed his spine without causing serious harm. Not so fortunate is the Regimental Medical Officer, Captain Montgomery, who is killed instantly by a bullet as he tends the wounded.*

*As day breaks, the Regiment is relieved by the Lincolns, but now their difficulties, and their casualties, mount. To extricate themselves, many have to crawl over the open space to the cover of the wood, and B and D Companies suffer heavy loss from rifles and machine-guns in enfilade. It is not possible to get our own machine-guns out, and Lieutenant Clairmonte remains, with his section, to rejoin the Battalion when he can. He and his men are never seen again.*

*Further orders from 3 Brigade follow.*

**From: 3rd Bde   To: 1 Gloucesters        PRIORITY**

**Bring your battalion to German first line trench South of BOIS CARRE aaa Bring from our lines as many bombs as possible including THRELFALLITE smoke hand grenades. Bombstores are in old Support Line.**

**C N Berkeley**

**Brigade Major**

The 28th move to their new position, and soon afterwards are withdrawn to a pleasant mining village, where they remain until 5 October, when they occupy a portion of the line running along the side of a long narrow wood. At the eastern end is a chalk pit. There are no support trenches, and the front line, much battered by incessant shelling, has a neglected appearance. Digging and revetting are now the constant occupation, and after the first evening the weather is dry. The issue of coke is abundant, so no one has to do without a fire.

The hostile shelling continues, and on the 8th it reaches a new pitch of intensity. In enfilade and from the front, the chalk pit and the trenches on either side of its salient are overwhelmed by a hail of 8 inch and 5.9 inch shells. Traverse after traverse is knocked in and flattened out. Casualties steadily mount. There is nothing to be done but await the infantry attack which must follow. The men bear the strain with remarkable calm. All communications are cut. At 1615 the shelling ceases, and at once the German infantry, issuing in dense masses from the Bois Hugo, advance against the Battalion, the main weight of their attack falling upon the chalk pit.

Immediately the Gloucesters are on the fire step, their rifle and machine gun fire cutting down the attackers. Now, the tables are turned, the erstwhile attacker has the luxury of being on the defensive; the supporting artillery joins in, and the enemy assault wavers then halts. Within minutes, the Germans are in retreat, scrambling for cover and trying, at great cost to themselves, to gain the cover of the woods. Wounded Gloucesters, stripped of their shirts to bind their wounds, join their comrades on the fire step; eager marksmen count aloud their hits.

In a cohort of heroes, Sergeant Biddle, the signalling sergeant, is outstanding. As a peacetime soldier he is reputed to have had a conduct sheet 'as long as your arm,' and in India was said to have thrown away his rifle and taken a drop kick with his topi when checked for some fault on guard mounting parade. His bravery is extraordinary and he will eventually become the holder of the Military Cross, the Distinguished Conduct Medal and bar, and the Military Medal and bar.

**War Diary (1915) of 1st Battalion the Gloucestershire Regiment (28th)**

**8th Oct. The Battn was relieved about 11 pm by the SWB, and on relief moved into support trenches east of the LOOS-LA BASSÉE road.**
**9th Oct. Shelling by heavy howitzers on support trench along line of LOOS-LA BASSÉE road. Casualties 1 killed, 1 wounded. From 7 pm to 1 am the Battalion was employed on the construction of our advanced saps running south from the fire trench immediately south of CHALK PIT WOOD.**
**10th Oct. Further shelling by Germans heavy artillery. Work continued on saps and trench heads south of CHALK PIT WOOD. Casualties 4 wounded.**
**11th Oct. Shelling of Support Trenches by day and night. Work on saps continued. Draft of 41 Other Ranks joined. Casualties, Lt L C BROWN killed, 2Lt S A WHITE to Hospital.**

OPERATION ORDER NO 31
by Lieutenant Colonel A.W. Pagan
Commanding 1st Gloucestershire Regiment
12th October 1915

The 1st Division will capture and consolidate the line of German Trenches from about H.19.a.8.0 to H.13.a.2.6 both inclusive, tomorrow the 13th.

The 1st Brigade will carry out the assault assisted by two battalions of the 2nd Brigade if required. The remainder of the 2nd Brigade will form the Divisional Reserve. The 3rd Infantry Brigade will hold the enemy to its front by rifle and machine-gun fire.

The artillery bombardment will commence at 12-30 pm tomorrow.

Gas and smoke will be discharged for one hour previous to the attack. Smoke only will be discharged in front of the 3rd Brigade. Smoke will be discharged by means of smoke grenades. OC Companies will arrange that 20 smoke bombs are placed in rear of every 10 yards of their front. One smoke bomb will be thrown on each 10 yards every 3 minutes from 1 to 2 pm. Bombs to be lit according to instructions in the box and to be thrown as far as possible to the front. Bombs will not be thrown in front of any portion of the line where the smoke is likely to blow back across our lines.

All ranks to wear smoke helmets rolled ready on the head by 12.45 pm.

At 2 pm the parapet will be manned and rapid fire opened at the German trenches where visible. This fire will be kept up during the whole of the assault and so long afterwards as firing comes from the enemy trenches opposite the Battalion. Every opportunity to be taken of firing at Germans retiring, and a sharp look out kept for counter attack.

Any German movement to our own front, either retirement or counter attack, to be reported at once to Battalion Headquarters by orderly if telephone is cut.

1st and 2nd Brigade bombing parties will carry red flags one foot square with horizontal white stripe. A look out for these flags to be kept once the assault has commenced.

sd. G.B. BOSANQUET, Captain
Adjutant 1st Gloucestershire Regiment

The attention of the Germans is attracted with complete success, and until dusk the regiment is most thoroughly trounced with high explosive shells. The poor condition of the trenches ensures that this causes many casualties, among them Captain Scott, commanding A Company, who is killed, and Lt Angier. The latter was wounded earlier in the battle, but refused to be evacuated, until hit seriously for the second time on the 12th.

Thus ends the participation of the regiment in the battle of Loos. Its total casualties are 5 officers and 63 other ranks killed, and 5 officers and 251 other ranks wounded. For weeks the 28th have dug and delved and fetched and carried in preparation for the battle; it has fared strenuously during the battle both in fighting and in fatigue; from the battle it has emerged with honour.

**Special Order of the Day by Commander 3rd Infantry Brigade**

Orders have already been issued by the GOCs 1st Army, 4th Corps and 1st Division showing their appreciation of the work done by the 3rd Brigade and attached troops on 8th October. The GOC 3rd Infantry Brigade also wishes to thank the brigade for their very successful action that day. In the 3rd Brigade the brunt of the fight fell on the 1st Gloucestershire Regiment. They stood the heavy shelling splendidly and were ready to meet the enemy with fire directly he advanced. The hard work they had previously done on their trenches helped much to lessen their casualties. The Artillery were also much assisted by a small party of the 1st Gloucestershire Regiment who volunteered to carry up ammunition over open ground that was being heavily shelled.

Afternote on the Battle of Loos by Lieutenant Colonel A W Pagan, Commanding Officer 1st Battn the Gloucestershire Regt (28th)

Had adequate reserves been available, the attack at Loos might well have resulted in a considerable victory. The assaults between Hulluch and the La Bassée road, after initial successes, were allowed to degenerate into dog fights with bombs, at which method of warfare the Germans, owing to their superior weapons, were our masters. But from Hill 70 to Hulluch, owing to the magnificent advance of the 47th and 15th Divisions, there was a definite break-through, and on 25th September, from 6.30 am until late evening, the Germans were certainly on the run.

If the 4th Corps had had a division close up in reserve to push through the gap, ignoring the gallant resistance of the troops opposed to the 1st Division, Hill 70 and Hulluch would have been occupied very early in the morning; had a strong reserve existed in the hands of the Army Commander and placed reasonably close to the battle, it is probable that the German reverse would have been really important. But however much the handling of the reserves that were available may be criticised, there is no doubt that the Commander-in-Chief was correct in his opinion that his armies were not strong enough for so large an operation as the Battle of Loos.

Extract from War Diary (1915) of 1st Battalion the Gloucestershire Regiment (28th)

28th Oct. A composite company of 5 officers and 200 other ranks under the command of Capt H.E. Wetherall paraded at LA BOUVRIERE with other units of the 1st Division for inspection by His Majesty the King. Battn beat the S.W.B at rugby by 20 pts to nil.

# Chapter 2

France
10th November 1915

Dear Mother

It is good to rest at last. We have had a week or two of quiet now, and we are back in a village which we know well, and where we are well liked, and the natives spare no pains in the interests of their lodgers. The estaminets are warm, even if the beer is weak, we have set up a regimental coffee shop, clean clothing has been issued, and everyone has had a bath.

In the afternoons there are numerous football matches of both kinds. We have twice beaten Welsh teams at Rugby football, and yesterday we just managed to beat an international side which the Staff Captain put up. The officers beat the sergeants 19 to 6, and I am proud to say I managed to get on and off the field in one piece!

Concerts are often held in a sort of village hall. Our Welsh comrades led the way, we reciprocated, and the third was a joint effort – marred by one of the entertainers who had too much to drink between his first and second turns, and could only be persuaded to leave the stage with difficulty!

Talking of concerts, I must tell you about one which was laid on a little while back. The Brigade Chaplain, a remarkable man, was the organiser, and he and I visited the chateau which at the time was a divisional headquarters to borrow a piano. We were received by a senior staff officer, who was not amenable to our request, and not keen on the idea of a concert at all. So the chaplain obtained a piano elsewhere, and had it transported to a wood near the headquarters. An invitation was sent to, and accepted by, the Corps Commander, to attend. The idea was that as soon as the staff officer heard the noise of the entertainment he would come rushing out, only to find a very senior general enjoying the concert. Unfortunately, our plot was betrayed by the weather, which was so bad that the concert was cancelled.

Last but not least, I am very proud to tell you that I have been made a member of the Distinguished Service Order. Of course, it is really an award to the whole Battalion, and I have made this point very forcibly – but I know how pleased you will be.

Your affectionate son
Alexander

# Gloucestershire Hero

**From the *London Gazette***

Alexander William Pagan, Major (Temporary Lieut-Colonel), 1st Battn The Gloucestershire Regt. For conspicuous good work when in command of his battalion, near Loos, on 8 Oct 1915, during a heavy bombardment of four and a half hours, followed by a heavy infantry attack. To be admitted to the Distinguished Service Order.

**War Diary (1915) of 1st Battalion the Gloucestershire Regiment (28th)**

**24th Nov. In trenches near LOOS. Enemy retaliated heavily to our bombardment. On our flanks we had on the right the 90th Regt of French Infantry, on the left the 2nd Welch. Lts Waddy, Hodges, and 2/Lts Heath and Lavender joined the Battalion. Party from 4th Royal Fusiliers visited for familiarisation in trench life, including one American officer serving in the British Army.**

**Report from the American officer:**

'I marvelled at the skill of our trench guide, who went confidently in the darkness, with scarcely a pause. At length, after a winding zig-zag journey, we arrived at our trench, where we met the Gloucesters. There is not one of us who does not have a warm spot in his heart for the Gloucesters. They welcomed us so heartily, and initiated us into all the mysteries of trench etiquette and trench tradition. In them I recognised the lineal descendants of the live Atkins, men whose grandfathers had fought in the Crimea, and their fathers in the Indian Mutiny. They were fighting sons of fighting sires, and they taught us more of life in the trenches in 24 hours than we had learned in months of training in England.'

# Chapter 2

⚜

France
26th December

Dear Mother

I must start by thanking you and all the ladies in England who helped to give us such a wonderful Christmas. We came out of the line a few days before the 25th, and enjoyed the luxury of moving by motor buses rather than on foot, to billets which we had occupied before, and where we were once again made most welcome. On Christmas Day, the officers served the men tea laced with rum, which they call 'gunfire', then at midday we gave everyone their dinners in the local school, half the battalion at a time. They really appreciated the seasonal fare which you and your helpers provided, especially the Christmas puddings, and gave three rousing cheers for 'All the ladies of the 28th for their kindness.' Eventually all the officers were able to sit down together for the first time since landing in France. Luckily there was a large room available, but even so we were all packed so closely together it was difficult to move our arms sufficiently to eat!

Today the holiday is over, and we are back in the line near a coal mine. Owing to the activity of the German artillery, the mine is only worked at night, when it is in full swing. Some of our men have visited the mine, and report that conditions are very different to those in the Forest of Dean.

It is now almost a year since I came out. We are all very cheerful, and determined to stick it until the end, but it is difficult not to see in the bigger picture that 1915 has been more successful for the Germans than for us. The Dardanelles affair did not go well, Serbia is out of the war, and we have not yet succeeded in delivering a really crushing blow here in France. No doubt wiser men than I are planning better things.

Please pass on my thanks, and those of ALL of us for the very splendid support you have all given, it means so much. Please thank Effie and Vi especially, I know what a great help they are to you. My warmest wishes for the New Year,

Your very affectionate
Alexander

As the year ends, the allied politicians and commanders are in earnest conclave as they consider their strategy for 1916. The French commander-in-chief, General Joffre, is constant in his belief that military decision is only to be found on the Western Front. Haig, who replaces French in command of the BEF in December, is of the same opinion. The meeting of the allied commanders at Chantilly agrees upon a simultaneous offensive on three fronts, but it quickly becomes apparent that this is not feasible. The British reinforcements of men and guns needed will not be ready before May.

Joffre tentatively selects a sector of thirty miles where the British and French lines converge, and the plan is put to the war cabinet on 28 December. The politicians are well aware what such an offensive implies; they are not blind to the loss of life which must follow, and not one of them gives his consent casually. But they are forced to face the hard fact that they must either consent to peace with the Germans in possession of almost all Belgium, much of northern France and the whole of Luxembourg, or they must fight on. If they fight, they must take the offensive, since they cannot hope to win by defensive means.

Joffre sets a tentative date of 1 July for the opening of the offensive, and on the 29th, Haig visits GQG, the Headquarters of the French commander-in-chief, where he agrees to cooperate. Planning begins for the Somme offensive.

# Chapter 3

January brings a new round of the familiar routine: so many days in billets in Divisional Reserve; so many days in Brigade Reserve; so many days as Battalion Reserve in third or fourth line trenches; so many days in the front line. As the New Year advances, a new lexicon comes into general use – the language of mining: Camouflets – the cavity made by an underground explosion which does not break the surface; galleries – the tunnels in which explosive is stored; sap and counter-sap, craters, clay-kickers and clay-kickers' mates, shafts, trolleys, dynamos and pumps.

**War Diary (1916) of 1st Battalion the Gloucestershire Regiment (28th)**

**14th Feb.** HARRISON CRATER mine blown. Working party sent to assist 2nd R Munster Fus in repairing trenches.
**17th Feb.** Enemy exploded mine at HARTS CRATER.
**19th Feb.** Bombing attack on HARTS and HARRISON CRATERS. 2 killed, 12 wounded, 5 missing.
**20th Feb.** Sap completed.

On 24 February, just as he is setting forth on a contemplative evening stroll, he is summoned to Brigade Headquarters; here he finds the Divisional Commander and the three Brigade Commanders with their staffs. Hart's Crater is considered a menace to the British line, and must be occupied without delay. Mines already prepared under the crater are to be fired at 1900 on the 26th, and the crater then seized and prepared for defence. The task is given to the 28th.

He goes forward on the 25th to look at the ground and prepare his plan. He needs 7 officers and 180 men; they are detailed and move forward to Regent Street, a trench lying east of the sunken road to Loos. Once the mines are blown, the two parties that are to make the posts on the edge of the crater will go straight to their objectives, hold the craters and begin fortifying them. They will be assisted by parties carrying sandbags filled with chalk, and others who will dig as fast as they can. He will personally lead the operation.

The mines are fired on time, and the Gloucesters are over the parapet and into the crater before the debris has settled. On the right, work begins immediately on digging, sandbagging and revetting. On the left, the crater is raked by machine-gun fire, and the party there reinforces those on the right. The weather is abominable, snow is whipped around the crater by a blizzard, and ice is forming on all exposed surfaces. Many of the 28th take bad falls, limbs are bruised and broken. Towards midnight the snow eases, and by the light of a bright moon a party of about 50 Germans can be seen advancing against the crater, their bayonets fixed. They are easily dispersed, the Lewis gun proving particularly valuable.

At 0715 the work is finished, the crater is secure and incorporated into the British line, and the Commanding Officer hands over to the resident unit. The operation has been a complete success, but the officer leading the left assault, 2/Lt Heath, is dead.

# Chapter 3

REPORT BY COMMANDER 3rd INFANTRY BRIGADE
ON OPERATIONS AT HART'S CRATER
NIGHT 25-26 FEBRUARY, 1916

The intention was to explode two mines under HART'S CRATER and then to occupy two posts on our lip of the crater, one on the right and one on the left. The operation was carried out by 200 men of the 1st Gloucestershire Regt under Lieutenant Colonel Pagan D.S.O.

The whole detachment was divided up as follows:

| TOTALS | |
|---|---|
| | 3 Bombers as covering party |
| 6 | 3 Bombers as diggers to dig the posts |
| 3 | Bombers as covering party |
| 6 | 3 Reserve Bombers for diggers |
| 3 | Reliefs of 10 men each as working party to dig communication |
| 30 | trench from our front line trench to the post on the crater |
| 42 | Second party as above |
| 20 | Reserve bombers to be used when necessary for either party and carry up bombs |
| 30 | 3 Reliefs of 10 men each as working party to dig communication trench round the top of the crater to join left and right post |
| 66 | Reserve |
| 200 | |

A reserve of 66 men was kept back in ENCLOSURE AVENUE about 400 yards behind. The remainder moved during the afternoon into the part of REGENT STREET to the left of the sunken road (immediately west of the CHALK PIT). A large supply of bombs had already been collected in REGENT STREET, and tools and rifle grenades were collected in the sunken road.

At 7.0 pm the mines were exploded. The operations were supported by heavy artillery fire on the enemy's trenches and by trench mortar and rifle grenade fire. By 5.15 am the post with splinter proof shelter and the communication trench from the front line to the post were completed.The whole operation was well carried out.

# Gloucestershire Hero

**I agree with Lieut Colonel Pagan's decision not to press the attack on the left as there was no cover to be obtained in this direction from machine gun fire.**

**H B Davies, Brigadier General
Commanding 3rd Infantry Brigade**

*France, 9th March 1915*

*Dear Mother*

*Winter is still with us, although every so often we have a bright, sunlit day. The big problem is the slush which is everywhere, soaking everyone's puttees, and leading to Trench Foot – if not carefully checked. Commanding Officers are held personally responsible for controlling this horrid complaint. The problem is that when out of the line large working parties have to be produced each night to dig and carry in slush and mud, and this makes it difficult to keep immune the tired men who are always soaked when they get back to their billets.*

*Leave has been stopped – we do not know why. No one expects leave during large operations, but the few men away during other times are of no consequence. Men are still required to do a year out here before they qualify – which is better than the French, for example – but if a few more leave boats were in service I am sure more could go. There is also, I am sorry to say, a perception that base personnel get leave more often than we, at the Front, do. It may not be correct, but I can tell you it causes much resentment.*

*Enough grumbling, I have to get it off my chest somehow! On the brighter side, I am happy to say that, within the Regiment, we are exceedingly well served by our administrators. You will remember that one of the first old chums I met when I came out was Quartermaster-Sergeant Hague, whom I know from South Africa days. He does extraordinarily good work. His round trip to bring up rations is at least 4 hours, and he never fails, come rain come shine. Orderly Room Sergeant Brasington is another stalwart, always up in the line with the regiment, and the first to catch up when consolidating a position. His knowledge and memory of men and events is remarkable. Regimental Sergeant Major Brain, solid, imperturbable yet unostentatious, and our Armourer Sergeant Grant, complete a remarkable quartet of Older Citizens who can always be relied upon, and who maintain an unshakable spirit in the 28th. I am lucky to command such men.*

*Your very affectionate son*
*Alexander*

**War Diary (1915) of 1st Battalion the Gloucestershire Regiment (28th)**

**6th March. Small camouflet exploded by 173 Coy RE under Gloucesters Observation Post on the DOUBLE CRASSIER about M4C74, destroying the galleries and counter-mine.**
**10th March. MAROC SECTOR. Heavy shelling along front line particularly A Company in 7thAVENUE round foot of Western end of NORTHERN CRASSIER. Trench wrecked, forward observation post on NORTHERN CRASSIER destroyed, also Sap leading up to it. In addition to H.E. shells enemy bombarded heavily with aerial torpedoes and trench mortar bombs.**
**12th March. Very heavy shelling throughout the day on A Company. At 7.25 am one dugout containing 25 men blown in on the CRASSIER. Working parties were trying all day during any little respite from the H.E. shells to dig through to them. Lt DURANT killed while in charge of the digging party.**

*To: Headquarters 3rd Infantry Brigade      From: 1st Gloucesters*

### RECOMMENDATION FOR THE AWARD
### OF THE VICTORIA CROSS,
### 16162 SERGT W.E.DRAKE, 1st GLOUCESTERS.

*On 12th March, A Company of 1st Gloucesters were occupying the DOUBLE CRASSIER, which came under very heavy shell fire throughout the day. At 715 am a dug-out containing 25 men under Sergt Drake, caved in. For 22 hours they worked to release themselves. Although strenuous efforts were made to dig through to them from above, these endeavours were in vain.*

*There was soon so little air in the collapsed dug-out that the slightest exertion proved exhausting, and many of the men were inclined to give up hope and effort. Sergt Drake however organised the whole party into reliefs, setting them to work with their entrenching tools for periods so short as to be within their powers; he cheered on or drove the faint-hearted according to their natures. By the courage with which he faced the situation, the skill with which he organised the work and above all by his dominating personality, he saved the lives of most of his men. Only six were dead when the emergence was made.*

*There is no doubt of the worthiness of his efforts, which I and other officers in the relief party witnessed in person. His conduct throughout was magnificent, in the very highest tradition of the Regiment and the British Army, and deserving of the very highest award. I recommend in the strongest possible terms that he be awarded the Victoria Cross.*

*A W Pagan, Lt Col, Commanding 1st Gloucesters*

In the ranks of the Allied High Command, a new name enters the equation, with major effect on military planning – Verdun. By the end of March, the savage series of German attacks on the fortress have caused 89,000 French casualties, and Joffre is seriously concerned that either it will fall, or his army will be bled white defending it. He appeals to Haig to take a major share of the planned offensive on the Somme, and agreement is reached.

The enemy's defences on the Somme are very powerful. During nearly two years of preparation, no pains have been spared to make them impregnable. The first and second systems each consist of several lines of deep trenches, well provided with bombing shelters and communications trenches. They are further protected by wire entanglements, many of them in two belts 40 yards broad, built of iron stakes interlaced with barbed wire, often as thick as a man's finger.

The woods and villages between these systems of defence have been turned into fortresses. Cellars and dugouts up to thirty feet deep provide shelter from artillery, and minefields and machine gun posts bolster the defences. Where our trenches run close to the enemy, observation of his front line is possible, and his second line and support lines are usually hidden. No easy task lies before any attacker.

The planning for the offensive is placed in the hands of General Rawlinson, with a three part aim: to relieve the pressure on Verdun; to assist Allies in the other theatres of war by stopping any transfer of German troops from the Western front; to wear down the strength of the German forces on the Western Front. Attrition is the key.

**War Diary (1916) for 3rd Infantry Brigade**

**3 April. Brigadier General DAVIES** proceeded to England on leave of absence. **Lieut-Colonel A.W. PAGAN D.S.O.** assumed command of the Brigade. Heavy day and night fatigues found by the Brigade. These include: 100 men working on the VILLAGE LINE in SOUTH MAROC, 200 men working on the communication trenches, various working parties for the R.E. and for mining and signal companies, sanitary fatigues at NOEUX, PETIT SAINT and LES BREBIS

**4 April.** The acting Brigadier reconnoitred the Support and Reserve Line and the approaches to the same, held by the 68th Brigade to our right.

**5 April.** The acting Brigadier reconnoitred the GRENAY-VERMELLES and GRENAY-NOYELLES lines. Heavy fatigues as usual. Baths allotted to battalions daily.

**6 April.** Acting Brigadier inspected the work on the VILLAGE LINE in SOUTH MAROC.

**8 April.** Fine day. Acting Brigadier went round Reserve and Support lines in MAROC sector prior to allotting work to Battalions.

**10 April.** Acting Brigadier went round all three lines in the Right Subsection.

Latest reports state that the Germans retaliated very promptly on our front line after the firing of the camouflet on SOUTHERN CRASSIER yesterday. Three aeroplanes passed over our front in the evening and dropped bombs on NOEUX-LES-MINES.

**Extract from War Diary (1916) of 1st Battalion the Gloucestershire Regiment (28th)**

10th April. 2pm. Our miners exploded a mine in between our sap and hostile sap on NORTHERN arm of DOUBLE CRASSIER. 100 feet of hostile wire was blown up and head of hostile sap destroyed, giving us a view for 30 yards (from our sap) up hostile sap. Hostile counter-mining galleries were destroyed.

On 14 April, while the 28th are reoccupying the Maroc Sector, the Germans blow a small mine in their own wire at the foot of the southern arm of the Crassier. Later in the evening this is investigated. At first it is difficult to account for, but when our tunnellers report four of their men killed in their nearest mine, it becomes clear that the crater is the outward and visible sign of a camouflet directed against that mine. The Germans are quickly at work trying to repair their wire. The 28th exercise their ingenuity over the next two nights to discourage them. First the Germans are driven to cover in their little crater amid the wire by rifle fire from the side of the Crassier, then they are bombed from the trench on top, overlooking the crater. As long as they continue in their efforts they are given a most uncomfortable time. Considerable skill in this respect is displayed by Lieutenant Lavender.

# Chapter 3

**War Diary (1916) of 1st Battalion the Gloucestershire Regiment (28th)**

**17th April. MAROC.** Enemy exploded a camouflet near the last crater formed on the SOUTHERN CRASSIER. This knocked out our mine gallery but did not affect our sap, and outwardly new crater appears as before.

## From the papers of Brigadier Charles Wilson

When our draft arrived at the Battalion in April '16, it was in the Chalk Pits, and my very first recollection of it when it came back to billets after a spell in the line was of men who were white from head to foot, just as if they had come out of a flour mill. From childhood I had been steeped in the traditions of the regiment, for my father had served in both battalions and I was born in the 61st, and I felt that I had achieved my greatest ambition when I found myself actually a member of the 28th.

I had been in Les Brebis only a few hours when I was ordered to take a working party up to the Battalion and had instructions to report to RSM Brain. It was then that I met the C.O. Lieut .Col. Pagan – known affectionately to all the men as 'Patsy'.

As he was the outstanding personality of the 28th for most of the nineteen months which I spent with the Battalion between April '16 and the end of the war, some description of 'The Little Man' as he was known to the officers is called for. Standing not much more than 5 feet and a few inches 'Patsy' looked more the build of a jockey than a Commanding Officer, and one could hardly have found a more contrasting pair physically than Patsy and his RSM 'Pop' Brain.

I hadn't been long in the Battalion before I learned that when 'The Little Man' was Adjutant he was reputed to have asked only two questions of every recruit when he inspected a new draft: 'Do you box?' and 'Do you play rugger?' It was some time after I joined the Battalion before either of the activities could be indulged in, but to see Patsy playing in a practice or inter-company game was a sight worth seeing. His bald head would be popping up here, there and everywhere, and on one occasion I remember seeing Ernie

Nash, an amiable giant standing about 6'3" and weighing about 16 stone, pick him up in his arms like a baby and gently deposit him on the ground.

When I look back on those days I cannot help wondering whether there was another battalion like it in the BEF. I am certain there wasn't a happier battalion or a better fighting battalion in the Army, and to Patsy must go the credit. He knew the history and indeed the regimental number of most of the men who had ever served with him in peacetime, and especially if a man had been outstanding in sport. At this time a large proportion of the battalion consisted of Regular soldiers and reservists recalled to the Colours.

There was no doubt about his efficiency as a C.O. and his courage was a byword in the battalion. Anyone who served under him could quote numerous instances of his utter fearlessness. At the time he appeared to be indifferent to the interests of his officers but this was merely that he expected his officers to be up to their jobs in every respect, and if an officer didn't measure up to his standard he soon got rid of him, but God help an officer if Patsy considered that he hadn't done all he possibly could for the comfort of his men.

France
8th May

*Dear Mother*

*I must tell you of a farcical situation which recently became a source of some anxiety. During our time in the last village, our stretcher-bearers occupied a cellar beneath a ruin on the main road. One day a patrol of Military Police appeared at the billet – contrary to the normally accepted rules of the game – and arrested the stretcher bearers for burning the woodwork of the house. The stretcher-bearers averred that their fire was made with derelict wood collected from the local area, and the police could not prove otherwise. I dismissed the charge.*

*But now higher authority – Divisional Headquarters no less! – fell*

*upon me for not supporting the representatives of law and order.
I was sure that I was in the right, as a result of which I admit that
my correspondence became a little heated. Finally, the Divisional
Commander himself stepped in and accused me of unduly prolonging
the war! I had to back down, and the whole thing is now forgotten –
and with no ill harm to the stretcher-bearers. I am sorry to say that
Bosanquet, our faithful Adjutant, leaves us today on promotion to a
staff post. He has been quite excellent, and I will miss him greatly.
You will also be interested to hear that C.A.S. Carleton is shortly to be
working with us. He started his career in the ranks of the 61st, where I
knew him well, and was commissioned in the Welch in 1907.*

*Our time recently has been filled with labour, working every night
digging, revetting and wiring. The men work with their usual energy
and good will – as long as that continues, all will be well.*

*Your very affectionate son*
*Alexander*

On Wednesday 31 May, President Poincaré, Prime Minister Briand,
War Minister Roques and Generals Joffre and Castelneau from
France meet Haig in the presidential railway carriage. Under the
impression that the French do not appreciate the efforts made by
British forces, Haig points out that in the five months of 1916,
British losses amount to 83,000 and that 653 mines have been
exploded. The main discussion centres on the need for an offensive
as early as possible.

Poincaré reports that he has just returned from Verdun, where
he has seen the senior generals. They tell him that losses have
been very heavy, and by the end of the month will reach 200,000.
They forecast that *'Verdun sera prise'*, and that operations must be
undertaken without delay to withdraw pressure on the fortress.

Haig would prefer to wait until mid-August, but under pressure
from the French, agrees to bring forward the date. On 1 July, the
Somme offensive opens, with very heavy British casualties.

The 28th are not involved in the first days of operations, but on 10 July they begin their forward move to the battle area. The men march well, their feet at last accustomed to the hardness of the pavé roads. There is a lull in the fighting at the moment, as battered divisions are replaced by fresh ones. The whole world is at Albert now. As one approaches it the activity always to be found in the rear area of a big battle becomes increasingly evident.

By 1945 the regiment is in its billets, between the church and the main Albert-Bapaume road. The billets are good, and the commanding officer and his headquarters occupy a house with a pleasant garden, abundantly stocked with redcurrant bushes, covered with ripe fruit. The town is occasionally targeted by German artillery, and battalion headquarters is lucky to escape injury when a shell bursts among its members in the garden.

Much time is spent in exploring the battlefield around Fricourt. The state of the enemy's trenches testifies to the power of our bombardment; the abundance of our guns is amazing. The mighty mine crater before Fricourt, the largest yet seen, is an object of wonder.

On the 14th, the commanding officer takes the company commanders to view the new position at Contalmaison, the rest of the battalion following at dusk. Contalmaison is one of the small communities that abound in this part of France, where there are no farms such as one finds near Bethune. The owners of a small tract of cornland dwell together in a little township, their crops growing right up to its edges; such places, two or three miles apart, are scattered over all the countryside. Each has its church, most have a chateau, but the village has almost disappeared.

The site of the church is marked by a great white stone; all that remains of the chateau is a vast cellar, now used as a dressing station. The other houses have disappeared.

Two days later, the commanding officer is ill-pleased to be summoned to Brigade Headquarters, sited in a cellar south of the village. Such a summons is usually an omen of strenuous things to come, and so it turns out. The Germans still hold the trenches north of Contalmaison, and it is the task of 3 Brigade to turf them out. The attack is ordered for 2200 that night, but the battalion commanders protest that they need more time for reconnaissance and preparation, and the hour is postponed until midnight.

**OPERATION ORDER**
**by Lieutenant Colonel A.W. Pagan, DSO**
**Commanding 1st Gloucestershire Regiment**
**16th July, 1916**

**Reference Map MARTINPUICH area.**

**The Battalion will attack between x.12.c.3.9. and x.12.a.1.61/2**
**2nd Munsters will attack on our left**
**2nd WELCH will attack on our right**
**S.W.B. will be in support.**

**Gaps in wire have been cut as shown to O.C. Companies.**

**Artillery fire will be as follows: from 11.50 pm to 12 Midnight, Intense bombardment of enemy's front and support line. From 12 M.N. to 12-5 am intense bombardment of enemy's support line. From 12-20 am barrage 200 yards from enemy's support line.**

**RED FLARES will be lighted by furthermost troops and by any troops who have reached their objective. Every officer will carry two flares.**

**Time of parade, B and D Companies 10-20 pm, A and C Companies 10-30 pm. B Coy on left, D Coy on right of front line, A Coy in 2nd line 100 yards to the rear, C Coy in third line 100 yards in rear of A.**

**Two extra bandoliers will be carried on each man. Four men in rear rank of each platoon of A, B and D Coys to carry one tool. Each man in C Coy to carry 10 bombs and one tool. Lewis guns – two with each coy.**

**Position of assembly – CONTALMAISON VILLA**

**Position of Deployment** – 150 yards in advance of position of assembly.

**Signal lamp in LOWER WOOD trained on S.E. point of CONTAILMAISON VILLA.**

**A Coy to make trained bombers up to 37, B Coy 27 and D Coy 22. Each bomber will carry 10 bombs in a bucket.**

> **sd. M A Green, Lieutenant**
> **Acting Adjutant, 1st Gloucestershire Regiment**

Everything is prepared in time though there is little to spare. The march and deployment are completed faultlessly. Heavy rain falls without ceasing, but everyone enters on the adventure light-heartedly and full of confidence. When the bombardment starts the leading troops are in exactly the right position; when the enemy's protective barrage falls on the Longueval Road, our troops are well clear.

The night is as black as it is possible to be. At midnight the advance starts, at first in quick time, then accelerating into a competition to be first over the enemy's line. The wire in front of the position is no obstacle, and little resistance is offered.

**Report on Operations on the night 16th July - 17th July 1916**
**Ref Map 57D SE 1:20,000**

**Battalion moved along CONTALMAISON-CONTALMAISON VILLA Road as far as CONTALMAISON VILLA, and then wheeled to the right and deployed along a wire fence running South East and parallel to the position to be attacked. 2 coys in front line in line of platoons in fours. 1 coy in support 100 yards behind, one coy in reserve 100 yards behind 2nd line.**
**Battalion then advanced to about 100 yards from position, and deployed into line, 2 ranks close order. Immediately the barrage ceased front line went through the 2 lines of enemy trenches to a position about 300 yards**

**beyond. 2nd line cleared and occupied enemy front and support lines, and
third line took tools to both other lines.**

**A trench was commenced where the battalion halted, but it was decided
to fall back to the German Support Line as our barrage showed no sign of
ceasing and prevented a further advance and was causing casualties. The
two German lines were then consolidated.**

**A.W. Pagan, Lt Col**
**C.O. 1st Gloucesters**

Patrols go out at dawn, but are stopped at once by hostile fire.
More than 150 dead Germans are found in the trenches. As they
belong to more than one unit, it is likely that a relief was in progress
when the attack took place. The enemy has left everything behind
him; the place is littered with rifles, greatcoats, head-gear and
equipment. The Gloucesters make use of abandoned greatcoats as
protection against the pouring rain. The casualties are three killed
and twenty-five wounded.

The value of the rehearsed attack is emphasised. Enemy
trenches, photographed from the air, are duplicated upon the
ground behind, and the planned attack rehearsed so often that the
men's mental task is simplified to that of merely getting himself to
the appointed place by a fixed time. It is difficult for anyone who
has not faced the mind-numbing terror of the assault to appreciate
that so far from making the movements wooden, they actually
engender greater elasticity, for the mind, released by discipline
and certainty from the pressure of fear, is able to think coherently
and thereby make adjustments for the unforeseen.

# Gloucestershire Hero

**SPECIAL ORDER BY BRIGADIER GENERAL H.R.DAVIES C.B.
COMMANDING 3rd INFANTRY BRIGADE**

The Brigadier wishes to thank all ranks of the 3rd Brigade for the splendid way in which they have performed their duty in the last few days. The success of the attack on the night of the 16th July was due to the excellent preliminary arrangements of Battalion Commanders, and to the dash and rapidity with which the attack was carried out.

Congratulations have been received from the Commander-in-Chief, G.O.C. 3rd Corps and G.O.C. 1st Division. Extracts from a report on the operation by 1st Division are forwarded for the guidance of all unit commanders.

Some 1,200 yards of 2 lines of trenches, both of which were wired, were captured, and held, by a night attack, with a loss of about 70 casualties. The success of this operation is to be attributed mainly to two factors. <u>Firstly</u>, that our most dangerous enemy, the machine gun (hidden, not in substantial emplacements, but in grass, hedges, shell holes, etc, where they are difficult to locate, and so destroy) was robbed of its power owing to darkness. Whatever fire they could bring to bear must be unaimed. <u>Secondly</u>, a short but very intensive bombardment by Field guns, which was followed <u>immediately</u> by the assault. The Infantry moved close up to the enemy's trenches under cover of the barrage, risked, and received, casualties from our own guns in order that no interval should elapse between the lifting of the barrage, and their entry into the trenches.

I would venture to suggest that positions, the attack of which offer exceptional difficulties by day, or even dawn, might meet with a greater degree of success if undertaken in the early hours of the night. Also that these hours might materially assist in the capture of a position the frontal attack on which promised to be very difficult and costly.

Wire-cutting was successfully accomplished during the day. The bombardment of the trenches began at 11.50 pm, and at midnight lifted on to the support line for another 5 minutes and then lifted again further back. The assaulting battalions got to within 150 yards of the enemy's trench by the time the bombardment began, and rushed forward at midnight. The trenches were not strongly held and the resistance was overcome at once with only slight casualties.

# Chapter 3

On 20 August, after a lengthy period in reserve, the 28th sets out at 1330 – a platoon at a time – to take over the line. Having arrived at Mametz Wood, it is stopped, assembled under cover there and ordered to relieve the 2nd/60th. The line is an odd place. It begins on the right with a small redoubt; further to the right after a gap of about 150 yards is High Wood, held in part by the Germans. The whole is battered beyond belief. The support line begins at the edge of the wood, and fades away to nothing after 200 yards.

It is plain that the German artillery will make the sojourn beside High Wood unpleasant. Headquarters and the forward trenches are plastered day and night with shells of all calibres up to 8-inch. Doubtless the enemy are having an equally unpleasant time, but this is no consolation when one is caught in barrage fire in the open. It is evident that the battalion layout must be changed as soon as the light permits, and at dawn two platoons of the support company are withdrawn to the reserve dugouts, and the remainder closed up towards the wood. Additional men are put into the sap, the safest place in the line, and a portion of the garrison of the front line are moved into shell holes a hundred yards forward.

When the 28th are relieved, after seven days under the heaviest artillery fire they have yet experienced, the front line is battered out of recognition, and the men, except those in the sap and the redoubt, are all out in shell holes. The relieving unit is a New Army battalion. It is commanded by a 56-year-old former regular officer who re-enlisted on the outbreak of war, and is now doing his job with the zest of a 2-year-old.

*On the morning of 4 September he attends orders at Brigade Headquarters with the CO of the 2nd Welch. The Brigade has been ordered to attack High Wood, an objective which for weeks has defied final capture. Again and again British troops have entered it, and for a time held their positions, finally having to fall back. The artillery of both sides has shelled the area so heavily that the wood exists only in name.*

*The 28th and the Welch are to lead the assault. The two commanding officers protest that an attack on such a narrow front cannot succeed; the wood can only be captured by occupying the ground on either side. Their protests are to no avail, and he goes forward to reconnoitre while formal orders are prepared at Brigade Headquarters.*

**3rd INFANTRY BRIGADE ORDER NO 44**

The 3rd Infantry Brigade will attack part of the German trenches in HIGH WOOD on the 8th September 1916.

The 2nd WELCH REGIMENT will attack from SAP 4 about S.4.c.6.61/2 to SAP 7 at the Western edge of HIGH WOOD. They will be responsible for the two German Communication trenches running North as far as the ride running from S.4.a.4.1 to S.4.c.1.81/2.

The 1st GLOUCESTERSHIRE REGIMENT will attack from the West from the New Trench, their objective being the two communication trenches running North from the two points mentioned above to the Northern edge of HIGH WOOD.

The 44th INFANTRY BRIGADE will attack the part of the first communication trench between the Northern edge of the wood and the Northern end of this trench at S.3.b.6.5. The 1st GLOUCESTERSHIRE REGIMENT will take over this bit of trench from the 44th Infantry Brigade when they have taken it. The 1st SOUTH WALES BORDERERS will place one company at the disposal of the 1st GLOUCESTERSHIRE REGIMENT for carrying tools, bombs, etc.

There will be a bombardment of the part of HIGH WOOD occupied by the enemy, beginning at 12 noon on the 8th September. During this bombardment the front line will be cleared from SAP 5 to SAP 7. The bombardment will cease ½ hour before ZERO, and the front line trench will then be reoccupied.

During the ½ hour before ZERO there will be a heavy bombardment with 2 in Trench mortars.

The Infantry advance will take place at ZERO. It will be covered by a barrage of 18 pounders, beginning at ZERO and continuing about 200 yards in front of our own trenches for 1½ minutes, thence lifting 100 yards every minute to a line about S.4.a.9.1, S.4.a.6.6, S.3.b.5.8.

The attack will be assisted by flammenwerfers. There will be a discharge of smoke over the enemy's trenches to the right of the attack, and over the North-East corner of HIGH WOOD if the weather is favourable.

ZERO will be at 6 pm on 8th September.

**Boer War** – Men of 2nd Gloucesters with local guide. *Soldiers of Gloucestershire Museum*

Sergeant Yarnall and heliograph detachment, 2nd Gloucesters. *Soldiers of Gloucestershire Museum*

Pagan with the winners of the inter-company shooting shield, 1907.

Regimental dinner, post Boer War. Centre table; far left, Wethered, who covered the advance at Paardeberg with the Maxims; second right, Pagan; far right, Foord, who 'behaved splendidly at Dewetsdorp'; top table, sixth from end, Lindsell, CO at Paardeberg, who led the 61st in the attack, despite being shot in the lungs. *Soldiers of Gloucestershire Museum*

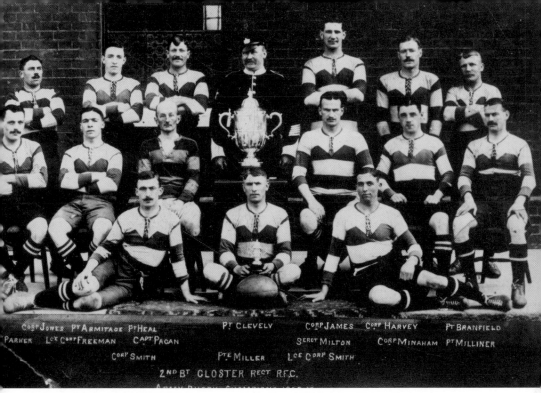

CORP JONES · PT ARMITAGE · PT HEAL · PT CLEVELY · CORP JAMES · CORP HARVEY · PT BRANFIELD
PARKER · LCE CORP FREEMAN · CAPT PAGAN · SERGT MILTON · CORP MINAHAM · PT MILLINER
CORP SMITH · PTE MILLER · LCE CORP SMITH
2ND BT GLOSTER REGT R.F.C.

The 61st team, winners of the Army Rugby Cup, 1910. Back row; Corporal, later Sergeant Major, James, scorer of the winning try, killed in France. Middle row; Pagan, 'his bald head would be popping up here, there and everywhere'; Corporal, later Sergeant, Minahan, about to be commissioned when he was killed at High Wood. Front row; Corporal, later Sergeant, Smith, who played for the Battalion in Malta and China, killed at High Wood. *Soldiers of Gloucestershire Museum*

Militia officers of 3rd (Special Reserve) Gloucesters, Pagan front right.
*Soldiers of Gloucestershire Museum*

Militia. Presentation of new colours, 1913. *Soldiers of Gloucestershire Museum*

Pagan, Adjutant, and Lieutenant Hartman, 3rd Gloucesters, 1914.
*Soldiers of Gloucestershire Museum*

**Great War** – The Gloucesters march through a French town on their way to the Front. *Soldiers of Gloucestershire Museum*

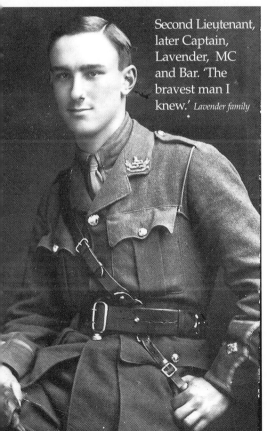

Second Lieutenant, later Captain, Lavender, MC and Bar. 'The bravest man I knew.' *Lavender family*

Lieutenant, later Captain, Baxter, MC. One of the longest surviving company commanders, he became acting CO after High Wood.

Captain, later Major,
Bosanquet, MC, 'a quite
excellent adjutant'.
*Soldiers of Gloucestershire Museum*

**Western Front 1915** – Gloucesters in the trenches. *Soldiers of Gloucestershire Museum*

Gloucesters snipers.
*Soldiers of Gloucestershire Museum*

A dug-out. *Soldiers of Gloucestershire Museum*

Captain Lavender's trench club. *Soldiers of Gloucestershire Museum*

Kindness to a German prisoner. *Taylor Library*

Battalion rear area, hot food being prepared. *Taylor Library*

The Somme battlefield. *Taylor Library*

Stretcher bearers. *Taylor Library*

Trench life. *Taylor Library*

A working party moves up. *Taylor Library*

German prisoners bring in
our wounded. *Taylor Library*

Out of the line, a chance to rest. *Taylor Library*

Waterproofs and waders. *Taylor Library*

The battlefield in winter. *Taylor Library*

Regimental Sergeant Major 'Pop' Brain, MC. *Soldiers of Gloucestershire Museum*

Regimental Quartermaster Sergeant Hague, MC. *Soldiers of Gloucestershire Museum*

Sergeant Major Biddle, MC, DCM and bar, MM and bar, with his family at Buckingham Palace, 1919. *Soldiers of Gloucestershire Museum*

**Dublin 1919** – loyal spectators at the July victory celebrations. Note the Union Flag. *Andrew Cusack*

**Dublin 1919** – troops search a car. *Constitutional Rights*

1st Gloucesters, 1924. Pagan, seated far left, company commander again.
*Soldiers of Gloucestershire Museum*

From right; Pagan; Orderly Room Quartermaster Sergeant, later Captain, Brasington, MC; RSM Ingram; Major, later Lieutenant Colonel, Carne, VC, Korean War hero; Lieutenant Colonel Gilmore, CO Depot, post 1945.
*Soldiers of Gloucestershire Museum*

Back Badge Parade, 1938. *Soldiers of Gloucestershire Museum*

Presentation of new colours.
*Soldiers of Gloucestershire Museum*

'Patsy', in full dress uniform.
*Soldiers of Gloucestershire Museum*

# Chapter 3

The drawbacks of the plan immediately become apparent. It is difficult to understand why the operation should take place, since a major assault is planned for a week later, which will inevitably lead to the capture of the whole wood. Why therefore attempt this sally into a small portion, fraught with hazard as it is? The coordination is likely to prove difficult; in the portion of the New Trench opposite the objective there is barely room for the two first assault companies. Supporting companies will either have to form up in the open, or await the departure of the lead companies before filing into the vacated trenches. The former alternative is overruled, which will inevitably result in a delay by the supporting companies in following up.

The 28th begin their forward movement at noon, A Coy, which is to be the forward right in the assault, leading. It is soon apparent that the faulty artillery work that has been observed during the preparatory work on the 6th and 7th is symptomatic of serious failings in the Royal Regiment. As they move forward B Company comes under the fire of our own guns, and howitzer shells which are intended to cut wire on the forward edge of the objective are bursting over New Trench. Among many casualties, 2/Lt Peake and Company Sergeant Major Hird are killed. The congestion in the trenches worsens, and it is several hours before the depleted battalion is properly organised.

The advance begins, on time, at 1800. A Company's left platoon is almost at once wiped out by enfilade machine-gun fire, but Captain Baxter, the longest surviving company commander, leads the remainder on to their objective, where they quickly consolidate. Now the shortcomings of the trench map on which the plan is based become apparent. What may have been trenches when the map was prepared are now unrecognisable in the tortured landscape, so torn by shell fire. B Company is held up by a group of Germans in a trench on the edge of the wood. A spirited charge overcomes them, but further casualties are sustained.

As soon as the two lead assault companies move off, C and D Companies start to follow, but movement down the trench is too slow. Conscious that it is the only way his men can be forward in time to support the Gloucesters up ahead, Captain Smith leads C Company into the open, followed by Captain Jones of D. They suffer heavily from the German artillery, alert to the danger. Both are wounded.

The position is taken, at fearful cost, but as the 28th begin the work of consolidating, it becomes obvious that they do not have the numbers to hold. Baxter is the first to call for reinforcements, but none are available. Further urgent calls are made by battalion headquarters, but by now the enemy's guns have the range to the Gloucesters' position, and in the unceasing storm of high explosive and machine gun fire, the Commanding Officer is wounded in the lower abdomen. He insists on remaining on the position until orders come from Brigade that they are to pull back to New Trench.

The reckoning is heavy. Six officers and 84 NCOs and men are dead, nine officers and 122 wounded, only Captain Baxter, Lieutenant Lavender, two other officers and 96 NCOs and men are unhit. This, for the 28th, is the end of the first phase of the Somme Battle.

Since its arrival at Albert on 14 July it has lost 546 officers and men.

**SECRET**

**3rd INFANTRY BRIGADE REPORT ON OPERATIONS**

**1. OPERATIONS**
At 6.0 pm on the 8th September 1916, the 3rd Brigade attacked the enemy trenches in the Western Half of HIGH WOOD.
**2. TROOPS ENGAGED**
2nd Welch Regiment on the right attacked from SAP 4, about S.4.c.6.61/2 to SAP 7 at the Western edge of the wood, against the enemy trench immediately to their front.
1st Gloucestershire Regiment on the Left attacked from New Trench against the enemy trenches inside the Western edge of the Wood.
1 Company South Wales Borderers was attached to the Gloucestershire Regiment. 3 Companies were in support.
**3. ZERO HOUR**
6 pm
**4. BOMBARDMENT**
Wire cutting along the Western face of the Wood was carried out during the

# Chapter 3

7th and 8th September. At 12 noon a slow bombardment (continuous) of the enemy trenches began until zero less half an hour. From -30 toZero there was an intense bombardment by 2" mortars.

## 5. <u>ASSAULT</u>

The attacking infantry left their trenches at Zero. On the right, the right company of the 2nd Welch Regiment gained their objective without much difficulty. The Left Company, however, were unable to progress owing to the Machine Gun fire from the North of the Wood, and fire from the enemy trench immediately in front of them.

The Gloucesters advanced to the edge of the Wood, and killed most of the Germans found in the trenches there. They then pushed on to the next line of trenches. This they found obliterated. The Germans in this neighbourhood appear to have been in small parties in shell holes surrounded by wire, and these had to be dealt with one by one. Casualties were heavy, but a few, including the Commanding Officer, managed to push on to the final objective which they occupied after a brisk hand-to-hand fight. Meanwhile the South Wales Borderers in support advanced from the trench from which the Gloucesters assaulted and pushed on through the Western edge of the Wood, but were hung up by fire, and were unable to reinforce the forward party of the Gloucesters, who at about 7.30 pm were forced to withdraw.

*Strict instructions have gone out from the C-in-C, repeated throughout the chain of command, that senior officers are not to place themselves in unnecessary danger. Too many generals have been killed leading their divisions and brigades, and now the order has gone down to commanding officer level. But where should he be? Unless reinforcements arrive, he is impotent. Marlborough and Wellington could shape their battlefield from the front. He cannot. All four companies have been committed, he has no reserve. Even if he has, how can he use them? It is not the job of the commanding officer to be up with the forward companies. But if not there, where? If the Battalion is to be reduced to a shadow, surely better to go with it than survive their destruction?*

*It is a problem without a solution.*

# Gloucestershire Hero

*The 36th Casualty Clearing Station at Heilly occupies a large farm, the barns and byres now converted into dormitories. Here the awful work of separating the wounded into 'hopefuls' and 'desperate' is undertaken. Doctors – officers of the Royal Army Medical Corps – move among the beds, which are close together. The light is shrouded, little is to be heard above the low mutterings of men to each other, or to the orderlies who strive to cater to their needs.*

*'Colonel Pagan, Sir? Cot 13 in this row, Sir. Conscious and able to sit up, but please do not converse for too long.'*

*'How long before he is moved on?'*

*'Two more days, Sir, it's the shortage of trains.'*

*Brigadier Davies moves slowly, uncertainly, to the small figure dwarfed by an enormous figure in the next bed.*

*'Patsy? How are you?'*

*'Good of you to ask, Brigadier, can't complain. No Freddy?'*

*'Dogs not allowed on the wards. How is the wound?'*

*'Bit painful but bearable. Bullet, not shrapnel, so less chance of infection. Not sure what the long term effects will be.'*

*'Long term, eh? Can you think that far? Will any of us live to see the "Long Term"? Someone told me the other day that any pre-war regular that comes out alive will have used up all his nine lives and more. You've been out for nearly two years now, this is your second wound is it not?'*

*'Never mind that, how is the Battalion?'*

*'In good heart, as always with the 28th.' A pause, and then, lowering his voice, 'What is left of them.' The Brigadier's voice drops to a whisper. 'Look, Patsy, I know it won't help much, but I wanted to pass on the Corps Commander's congratulations, and also one from General Strickland. He asked me to tell you that it is not just for this show, but for all you have done. You know he doesn't lob out strawberries easily. I just wanted to say that I could never ask for a better battalion, or a better C.O. They will have a chance to settle down now. That fellow Baxter is very sound, he will command until you are fit. But they need you back, Patsy.'*

*'They need you back. They need you back. They need you back...' The train repeats its refrain as it crawls along the congested lines. 'They need you back. They need you back.' But return to the 28th must wait. While the Gloucesters move to a quiet area and slowly absorb*

# Chapter 3

reinforcements, he is conveyed along the well worn path; from Casualty Clearing Station to Field Hospital; from Field Hospital to Base Hospital; across the Channel to convalescence in a comfortable country house in England. Here he receives news from the Battalion, and he can absorb the loss of so many friends and comrades.

His thoughts turn often to those he has known so well, now gone. Sergeant Gray, whose grandfather and uncle were Quartermasters of the 28th, and whose father was Regimental Sergeant Major; Sergeant Griffin, who refused the offer of a home posting so that he could remain with the 28th in France; Lance Corporal Sudbury, who refused a commission so that he could go to the 28th at the post of danger; the light-hearted Sergeant Sibthorpe; Sergeant Daniels; Sergeant Strong; Corporal Fortey; Company Sergeant Major Ritchings. So many good men, such strong hearts, such pride, such loyalty.

He thinks of the rugby players; Company Sergeant Major James, the giant hero of the Army Cup, and his team mate from 1910, Sergeant Minahan, about to take up a commission when he was killed on the Somme; Private Yearsley, whose promise as a wing three-quarter was just beginning to show; Corporal Sayer, from the Depot XV; Sergeant Smith 42, who played for the Battalion in Malta and China, and Sergeant Murray, stand-off in the Battalion XV. All gone, all gone...

He thinks of Sergeant Drake, DCM, and his extraordinary heroism, of the officers who have gone uncomplaining to their deaths at the head of their men. He cannot fail them.

'They need you back. They need you back. They need you back...'

3rd Infantry Brigade Operation Order No 40

**1. The 3rd Infantry Brigade will march into billets in FRANVILLERS on the morning of 12th September.**

**2. For march purposes the undermentioned will count as one unit**
**Brigade Headquarters and 2nd Royal Munster Fusiliers 2nd Welch Regiment and 3rd Machine Gun Company 1st Gloucestershire Regiment and 3rd Trench Mortar Battery...**

# Gloucestershire Hero

Arundel Ward
Lady Carnarvon's Hospital
48 Bryanstone Square
London W1H 2EA
3rd October 1916

Dear Baxter

Many thanks for your very kind letter. I am in good hands and good spirits. This hospital is really rather fine. It was originally established at Highclere by the Countess of Carnarvon, paid for by Baron Rothschild. Last year it moved here, to London, a lift was installed, operating theatre, X-Ray apparatus, and all the stuff for a first class show. There are about forty beds, and the wards are all small. I share with one other chap, and the service is extraordinary. I get breakfast in bed, and a footman then takes my order for papers!

My wound is well on the way to healing, and I hope to be back with you in about a month. In the meantime, I know you will take good care of the battalion, although I believe Pusey Vinen will be back with you to take over before long.

Everyone did so well in the High Wood affair, we did not let the Regiment down. The Brigadier came to see me at the CCS, and was very complimentary. I did emphasise to him that you all need a really good rest, a chance to absorb BCRs, and to retrain. He did not need persuading. I am delighted that you are getting the opportunity for sport. Good luck with the rugby!

Yours ever,
Alexander Pagan

**Extract from 3rd Brigade Order No 62**

**The three Battalions of the 3rd Brigade will move to MAMETZ WOOD tomorrow, 1st November... This move is in relief of three battalions of the 143rd Brigade, working on roads under the Chief Engineer...**

'Shall I lock the carriage doors, Sir?'

'Good Lord, why?'

*Sergeant Lloyd looks embarrassed.* 'It's the rumours, Colonel, the old hands tell the new recruits stories, and then they get the wind up. Plus, Sir, begging your pardon, a lot of the new ones are not volunteers, not like we were. They hear about this crucifixion business, and they decide they don't want to go to France.'

'I see. I have heard the rumours, but in my opinion, that is all they are – rumours. The Hun can get up to some pretty awful behaviour, but not that. It all started with the Canadians, then it was the Dublin Fusiliers, but when the story was checked, they found that the place where one of our chaps was supposed to have been fastened to a barn door with bayonets was never part of the German line. So forget it. I will have a word with the draft. The regiment is in reserve at present, so they will have a chance to settle in and train. Most of them are going to D Company, under Captain Lavender. He is a first class officer, he will see them right.'

'I heard from the RSM that we are making roads now. What will they make us do next?'

'It is hard work – 5.30 in the morning until 11, then noon to 3 pm. But it gives everyone a chance to shake down together, and living in tents for a week or two will toughen them up. But don't lock the doors, they will not let the 28th down.'

*Sergeant Lloyd hopes fervently that the CO is right. He has lent a pound to Private Whitman on the promise that he will return it – and himself – when he has 'sorted out a bit of a problem with his missus and a munitions worker' he has heard about. His faith is justified; just as the boat train is about to pull out, a very sweaty Whitman is hauled aboard.*

*Sergeant Lloyd notices that his knuckles bear the perfect imprint of a set of teeth.*

**3rd Infantry Brigade War Diary (1916)**

**10 November. In morning 1st Gloucesters moved up to MAMETZ WOOD in relief of the South Wales Borderers. In the evening Lieutenant Colonel PAGAN returned from sick leave and stayed the night at Brigade HQ.**

**11 November. Brigadier General Davies and Lieutenant Colonel Pagan motored up to MAMETZ WOOD. A quiet day.**

**19 November. In the morning Brigadier General Davies carried out a small tactical training exercise on ground between MAMETZ WOOD and BAZENTIN LE PETIT WOOD.**

*There are some twenty officers on the little hill between the two woods. They take advantage of the weak autumn sunlight, sitting in clumps in the lee of the shattered remnants of what had once been fine oak and stalwart beech. They are safe here, the war has moved on, and this place of ill fame, scene of such bitter fighting, is now an object of curiosity. A broad gauge railway line is nearing completion up Caterpillar Valley, and hutted camps are springing up just below them. Captain Lavender finds himself in unaccustomed proximity to his Commanding Officer, newly returned from convalescence. They exchange news, of families, of old comrades, of war and rumours of war. There are other rumours: that Australian deserters inhabit the huge dugouts in Mametz Wood, emerging at night to forage; that the leave scheme is to be extended; that the leave scheme is to be cut short; that allowances are to be increased; that allowances are to be reduced.*

*Lavender, emboldened by the relaxed mood of the morning, pulls out a hip flask.*

*'Colonel, would you be offended if I offered you some rum and coffee?'*

*'Offended, certainly not!'*

*They all scramble to their feet as the Brigadier arrives.*

*'Stand easy, everyone, and do sit down. You may wonder what on earth we are up to, meeting here like a works outing. The fact is I have some bad news – bad for me that is. I shall shortly be leaving the Brigade after almost two years. It has been a huge privilege to command one of the most senior formations in the Army, composed almost exclusively of Regular units. You have shown the standards that we expect of such units, and I have asked each one of you here today because you have – every one of you – done something very special to uphold the honour of your Regiments. I wish there were more of you here, but the efforts of the last few months – efforts that are recognised by the French nation as much as by our own – have sadly depleted our ranks. God knows what awaits us in the future. This beastly war will not end this*

*year, nor next, but we will stick it out. I know that. Gentlemen, you are the bravest of the brave, and I leave you with a heavy heart, but confident that the future is in good hands. Now, if Sergeant Olive will bring it on, there should be a small offering of food and drink to pass the time.'*

On 27 November, the 28th return to the line. The trenches lie in the low ground near the Albert-Bapaume road. Mud is everywhere, and the way up is long and wearisome. As soon as they leave the road the going becomes appalling. By an unusual oversight, the men go up to the line in gumboots, instead of boots and puttees. When some plunge into the trench system at Pioneer Alley, they are stuck in the mud before they have gone a hundred yards. They have to be extricated by being hauled out from above, after dark.

The trenches, when the remainder reach them, are knee deep in glutinous mud, without parapet, parados, board or firestep. In places there are quagmires, two or three hundred yards across, between platoons. Gum boots are soon left in the mud, and men remain bootless until a supply can be brought forward next evening.

In such evil conditions, cooking is impossible. The rations come up nightly, on trucks pushed by fatigue parties from the reserve battalion. It is so difficult to identify friendly from enemy positions that two Prussian guardsmen walk into the front line trench from behind. On Christmas Eve, the 28th are directed to dig a new trench behind Yarra Bank. It is to be a good trench, at least four and a half feet deep, with solid traverses and proper fire steps. The whole battalion sets off in a night of pelting rain and a tearing gale. Work starts at 2300, and after five hours they return, soaked, to their trenches. The trench is named Gloucester Trench.

On the 29th the Battalion moves into quarters at Becourt camp. On the 31st a reinforcement of 175 men arrives; they are all former members of the Royal Engineers or Army Service Corps, transferred to make good the huge losses in the infantry during the Somme offensive.

Christmas dinners are eaten on 4 January 1917.

# Gloucestershire Hero

*France*
*5th January 1917*

*Dear Mother*
*Again, we must thank you and the friends of the Regiment, from the bottom of our hearts, for our splendid Christmas fare. We could not sample it until yesterday, but we enjoyed it the more for the delay. The men dined in relays, since we only had 300 plates, and were very happy with all the good things you had sent, and the turkeys and beer which we bought with the very generous money from you all.*
*Believe me, we do appreciate that life is not easy for those at home. In many ways, because of the constant anxiety you all have for your loved ones, your existence is probably more prone to heartache than ours, yet the endless supply of parcels never ceases. Please accept my thanks, dear Mother, and pass on my great gratitude to Vi and ALL the friends who have contributed so much. It will never be forgotten.*
*I must close now; the General is on the prowl!*

*Yr very affec son*
*Alexander*

**From the papers of Brigadier Charles Wilson**

'One might well wonder how the battalion ever recovered from the huge losses of the Somme battles. That it did and was brought again to peak form by 1918 was due to the genius of leadership in a little man not much over five feet in height – Lt.Col. A.W. Pagan.'

# Chapter 4

'The decision to retreat was not reached without a painful struggle. It implied a confession of weakness, bound to raise the morale of the enemy and lower our own. But as it was necessary for military reasons, it had to be carried out.'

General Ludendorff, Chief of the German Imperial General Staff

The retirement of the German Army to the Hindenburg Line is a triumphant vindication of Haig's Somme offensive. Their army has been so worn down that it has to adopt a shorter line, abandoning, for the first time, French territory which it has occupied since 1914. The coming year is to see a cautious advance by the British to the new positions, a disastrous campaign by the French General Nivelle, ensuing mutinies in the French Army, and the appalling conditions of Third Ypres, or Passchendaele. In a year so difficult for the British Army, the 28th are more fortunate than many: they are to be involved in a highly secret operation to make an amphibious landing on the coast with the intention of neutralising the German U-boat base at Zeebrugge.

This all lies in the future, as the Battalion moves to billets in Contay in an exceptionally cold winter. There are twenty degrees of frost on the night of arrival, and thirty-eight degrees three nights later. They are lodged in barns, which can only be warmed by purchasing trees for fuel. The commanding officer's concern is to mould his newly formed unit into a coherent whole, and he directs that hard training be carried out on the undulating frozen ground. After a little company training, the battalion attack is practised on several days. The time spent at Contay, where they can pursue their own course, does a lot to pull the regiment together, and the 28th begins to approach its proper standard for the first time since it's wreck on the Somme.

At the end of January, the 28th returns to the line south west of Peronne. The familiar routine of trench life is resumed; so many days in the front line, so many in support, so many in reserve. Sometimes the billets and trenches are well constructed and clean, sometimes, as at Telegraph Camp, they are indescribably filthy. In February, instruction is given in a new way of combating Trench Foot. It is badly needed.

A new position at Barleux has to be reached by a communication trench over a mile long. The front line consists of two trenches joined by shorter communication trenches equipped with sufficient deep dugouts to hold everyone in comfort. A raid on the German first and second line trenches is ordered by 3 Brigade Headquarters.

*'Let's hear your report, Granger.'*

*Second Lieutenant Granger, grimed from head to foot in mud, is laden with German bombs, ammunition and an entrenching tool. He pauses to gather his thoughts.*

*'I went out to look at the ground for the raid, Colonel, while the rehearsals were continuing. It was strange, I could hear nothing from Fritz, so I slowly crawled closer to his line, stopping every few yards to listen. Sometimes, the mud was so bad that I had to stand for a few paces. I thought I would give it a go, so I eventually reached his parapet – here at about S.14.d.2.'*

*He and Granger peer at the trench map. The point indicated is indeed the exact objective detailed by Brigade for the raid.*

*'I got into the trench by sliding in, but by this stage it was so difficult to move through the mud, that all I could do was examine the bit around me, and pick up a few souvenirs – I thought the Int chaps might find them useful. I had the Devil of a job getting out of the trench, I had to make steps up the side and then pull myself up.'*

*'So you saw no sign of enemy in the position?'*

*'None, Colonel, and I think I know why. The fact is it is such an awful bit of ground that they obviously decided to evacuate it. If the raid goes ahead, we will hit air, and then be left stuck, literally, in the mud.'*

# Chapter 4

*'Well done, Granger, an excellent bit of initiative, and a most useful report. I shall have a word to Brigade about the operation.'*
*The raid is cancelled.*

On 4 March, Gloucester meets Gloucester. The 28th relieve the 10th Battalion, spend a few days in the line, are relieved, and on the 15th are back in the line when intelligence is received that the German withdrawal to the Hindenburg Line is about to begin.

**3rd INFANTRY BRIGADE ORDER NO 93**

The enemy in front of us is reliably reported to have withdrawn the bulk of his forces East of the River SOMME, and to be holding his front line with not more than 20 men per Company.

The Brigade Commander intends to penetrate the enemy's line tonight (up to and inclusive of his Support Line) in two or more places and to consolidate and hold the ground gained.

For this purpose two separate enterprises will be organised. The enterprise on the Left of the Brigade Front will be undertaken by the Officer Commanding 1st Gloucestershire Regiment...

The Officer Commanding 1st Gloucestershire Regiment will arrange for three gaps in the hostile wire to be cut between N.17.c.5.0 and N.23.a.5.9 at such time as he may decide before ZERO hour.

At ZERO hour, three parties of 8 other ranks, the whole under the command of an officer, will pass through the gaps in the wire and occupy the front line German trench between the points above mentioned.

On gaining an entry into the German front line, they will at once be supported by two platoons previously detailed for the purpose.

No artillery preparation will take place.

ZERO hour will be arranged by the Officer Commanding 1st Gloucestershire Regiment at any hour before 12 midnight 16th/17th March.

*The affair starts on time. The party, under Second Lieutenant Granger, leaves the 28th's trenches and proceeds stealthily along a ditch towards the enemy. For a long time they move without check, until, having found their way through the wire, they are on the German parapet. Suddenly the silence of the night is riven by the clatter of machine guns and the explosion of bombs. The patrol scatters, and a slightly wounded member scurries back to report the situation.*

*He decides that he must take command on the spot, and moves forward to the wire with a small party. He finds Granger badly wounded, and two others less seriously hurt. They can be moved on the backs of the relief party, but Granger is delirious and crying out directly any attempt is made to move him. Private Barker volunteers to stay with him, and eventually brings him in before daylight, but Granger dies. Others of the party return by the wrong route to the 28th line, to be met with a Mills grenade. Fortunately the only harm done is to the skirt of Captain Lavender's macintosh.*

*He moves slowly back down the difficult going of the trenches to find the General Officer Commanding the 1st Division on the telephone. Orders from Brigade follow.*

**3rd INFANTRY BRIGADE ORDER NO 94.**

**The 1st Division has orders to occupy the main VILLERS-CARBONNEL-STERPIGNY Road.**
**The 1st Gloucestershire Regiment will hold and consolidate the line of the ISAR TRENCH from 0.19.c.4.5 to N.30.a.5.2 and will push forward patrols and establish observation posts on the line of the EGLANTINE TRENCH from 0.25.b.9.9 to 0.25, Central. One company 1st South Wales Borderers is placed at the disposal of O.C. 1st Gloucester Regt.**
**Front line Battalions will push out patrols down to the river within the Brigade area.**

Shortly after 0800 both patrols are successful: the one on the left meets with no opposition while the one on the right quickly overcomes the slight resistance it encounters. The leading companies quickly occupy the front and second lines and continue the advance. There is no sign of any enemy. Soon, the whole battalion is on the move, 'shaken out' in the approved formation, a chance for forward junior commanders to take the initiative. By 1300 the Divisional objective is reached, and the 28th occupy Isar Trench, while pushing forward outposts 800 yards ahead. The Somme is in sight, liaison is established with the two flanking battalions, and, apart from some desultory shellfire, all is calm.

The enemy has not left without a sting in his tail. Booby traps are suspected and one is found: a chair with a line tied to it which leads to a sticky bomb. Although all the bridges have been destroyed, a patrol under Second Lieutenant Forbes finds a small boat, crosses the river and pushes on for a couple of miles. There is still little sign of the enemy. Their withdrawal to the Hindenburg Line has been completed.

RSM Brain returns from convalescence, and ensures that a thorough inspection by the new brigade commander passes off well. Routine administration is the order of the day for the next few weeks, until, on 27 May, the 28th entrain for the Ypres area. Very few of those who had detrained eleven months earlier go with it.

The Battle of Messines Ridge is an offensive whose strategic objective is to reduce pressure on the French Army, which has suffered over one million dead. The tactical objective is to capture the German defences on the high ground south of Ypres. This ground dominates the area from which the British High Command intend to advance to Passchendaele, then capture the Belgian coast up to the Dutch frontier.

The task of the 28th is to carry trench mortars and their ammunition to the front and support-line trenches east of St Eloi, and the whole battalion is on fatigue duty day and night. They return to their camp before the opening of the battle, in which nineteen enormous mines are detonated. The explosions can be heard at Meteren, where they are quartered, and from where the Battalion is ordered forward at short notice to clear the battlefield. They work under the direction of a young field company commander of the Royal Engineers, a fellow Old Cheltonian named Pakenham-Walsh.

The work is strenuous: making roads and laying water pipes, preceded and followed by long marches to and from the work area, but they have time to marvel at the huge craters left by the mines that had been exploded immediately before the attack. Ypres, itself, is completely wrecked. It is during a short break for a meal towards the middle of June when commanding officers are summoned to Brigade Headquarters for what the Brigadier calls a 'pow-wow'.

*The Commanding Officers gather at the pleasant farm house which is the temporary headquarters of 3 Infantry Brigade. The Brigade Commander is in a sombre mood. His first words reveal why.*

*'What I have to say is highly secret, and for the moment is to go no further than yourselves. The authorities are doing their best to hush it up, but God knows it's bound to get out, especially when the politicians get hold of it. The situation is extremely serious: the French Army has mutinied.'*

*The Brigadier pauses for a moment while gasps of surprise mingle with the odd oath.*

*'Of course, we do not know the full extent, and up until a day or so ago it was being denied completely. But now we know the outline facts. On 27 May, some 30,000 French soldiers left the front and marched to the rear. By 7 June, some fifty divisions, about forty per cent of the Army, were affected. They are showing no violence to their officers, they are simply saying that they will take part in no further offensives.*

*'There seem to be three threads to all this. The first is the failure of Nivelle's much publicised offensive. Unfortunately he promised far more than he could deliver, and their Army now lacks confidence in their leadership. Second, the Revolution in Russia is undoubtedly having an effect. The spirit of Bolshevism is abroad, and hotheads are rabble rousing. The third factor seems to be the simple one of leave. They are just not giving leave to their men.*

*'Now, you will all have already worked out the consequence of all this for us. We shall be the only ones on the Western Front doing the fighting, and until the French authorities can get a handle on the situation, we shall have to do the heavy lifting.'*

*A chorus of questions: 'Will they shoot the ringleaders?', 'Who is in charge of sorting it out?' is broken by the Commanding Officer of the Gloucesters.*

*'I think we should take the business of leave to heart. At present it takes sixteen or seventeen months for a man in the ranks to get leave, which is deplorable. He gets pretty shirty when he sees that every squirt who wriggles into a safe job far behind the line gets his leave often and regularly. The system should be changed.'*

*Growls of approval from the other Commanding Officers show their agreement.*

*'Alright, Patsy, that is not what we gathered to discuss, but you have a point. I will take it up with Division, and see what we can do. Meanwhile, remember, not a word about the French.'*

One of the moves resulting from the disturbances in the French Army is their replacement on the left of the British Expeditionary Force where they held the shoreline. Here they are replaced by the 1st Division, and in early July the 28th move into reserve in the sector on the east side of the River Yser. The ground is sandy, and with the river flowing only 600 yards to the rear, the front line is vulnerable to shell fire, and lacking in depth.

The Regiment is fortunate not to be one of the two front line battalions when the Germans open an intense bombardment of their positions. The shell fire increases in severity throughout the following three days, until on the 10th the Germans attack, overwhelming the few survivors.

Late in the evening, while he is temporarily in command of 3 Brigade, the Battalion is placed under command of 2 Brigade, and two companies, under Captain Lavender, are moved to Nieuport Bains. They are shelled heavily, and four officers, among them Captain Lavender, are wounded. He has commanded D Company for nearly a year, and has been a byword for calm courage and inspiring leadership since he joined the 28th in November 1915.

Alarms of fresh German attacks are plentiful over the next few days, and every night enemy planes bomb the dunes. On 17 July, the 28th moves to Le Clipon Camp.

While the British Army prepares plans for the offensive in Flanders which is designed to take the weight of the German Army off the French, the 28th embark on an extraordinary adventure.

The high ground which stretches from Messines towards Passchendaele is to be the main objective of the campaign which comes to be called Third Ypres. Another thread of the evolving Allied strategy is a plan to neutralise the German submarine base at Zeebrugge on the Belgian coast. This could be achieved if our heavy artillery can be moved in to a position from which they can bring it under sustained fire.

The plan is for the 1st Division – 1, 2 and 3 Infantry Brigades and supporting arms – to make an amphibious landing once the Fifth Army has gained sufficient ground to support it. The division will land at dawn behind the German line, while the XVth Corps makes a simultaneous attack from Nieuport and Nieuport Bains in a north-easterly direction. One brigade is to land at Westende Bains, one at Middlekerke Bains and one in between. Immediately after landing, the tanks are to drive straight up the sea wall followed by the two leading battalions; they will protect the landing of the remainder while two tanks deal with any strong points. The whole force will then push inland, beyond the Nieuport-Bruges Canal, while a strong party, composed of cyclists and a motorised machine gun battery supported by infantry and sappers, will seize and destroy the batteries at Raversyde. This will protect both the subsequent landing of our heavy guns, and the advance of XV Corps.

Each brigade is to be transported by a pair of monitors – Royal Navy ships of shallow draught mounting heavy guns up to six inches calibre – with, lashed between them, pontoons 200 yards long and ten yards wide. The guns, stores, ammunition, three tanks and two infantry battalions are to be carried on the pontoons, the remainder of the troops on the monitors. Each brigade is to be accompanied by its trench mortar battery, a field company of Royal Engineers, artillery, tanks and supporting services.

The monitors will first arrive in position, prepare their pontoons and load their stores. At dusk the infantry will embark, and at dawn the next morning the force will sail in time for a dawn landing, concealed by a smoke screen laid by small craft as far as the Dutch frontier. The heavy guns of the monitors will provide covering fire for the landing.

The sea wall is a serious obstacle, with an average slope of one in two, in places steeper. The plan depends for success on the perfect execution of each succeeding stage – a questionable hypothesis – and on the utmost secrecy, and the 28th are housed in a closed camp on the coast at Le Clipon. It is surrounded by a strong fence which is constantly patrolled, with guards at the entrance. The only horses inside are chargers and a few draught horses. The transport is camped two miles away; when it brings the daily mail and rations, it dumps them, then departs, without contact with the inmates. A rigorous censorship greatly delays the despatch of mail to England, and secrecy is further tightened by releasing few details of the planned operation to unit level. No one who is not connected to the operation is allowed in, although home leave is permitted. This luxury perhaps results from the commanding officer's appeal, but it has a risk. 'No one objects to leave, but although every man going on leave is personally warned never to mention where he is or why, yet human nature being what it is, how could the average soldier refrain from telling his mother all about it.'

The camp, pleasantly situated among the sand dunes, and near to lovely beaches, becomes known as the 'Hush Camp.'

A new order of battle is required to meet the strange circumstances. Battalion Headquarters is to include the Company and Regimental quartermaster sergeants, as well as the signallers, pioneers and medics, to a total of six officers and sixty-five men. Each of the four companies is of five officers and 165 other ranks, and eighty-eight hand carts are allotted to each battalion in place of the normal horsed transport. Each rifleman will carry 170 rounds of ammunition, rifle grenadiers will carry seventy rounds of ball and ten rifle grenades, and each bomber sixteen Mills bombs in addition to ball ammunition.

Everyone works extremely hard. After battalion drill on the shore and breakfast, work consists of practising embarkation, disembarkation and the ascent of the sea wall. Full sized plans of the monitors and pontoons are laid out on the sand so that all may become accustomed to their positions. The Battalion thrives on the hard physical training, and enjoys the sense of purpose which this unusual exploit encourages. Ideas spring from all ranks; one of the most important is that scaling the sea wall demands a good grip, and that newly nailed boots give the best results.

After training, there is plenty of time for sport, not least the wonderful bathing which the sandy beaches and warm seas afford. Jelly fish are a hazard, but the best cure for their stings is a half hour of hard rugby training. The team includes the commanding officer, Sergeant Armitage and Private Miller, members of the 61st's winning side of 1908, and Quartermaster Sergeant Nash and Corporal Nash from the 28th's first team. They sweep all before them, victories made doubly sweet because their opponents include three Welsh battalions. At soccer, they are winners of the Brigade cup, but lose to the Loyals at Divisional level. Cross country, boxing and athletics complete the range of enjoyable sports which help to weld the Battalion into a well trained unit with high morale.

Unfortunately, events elsewhere determine their future: the Fifth Army, after three months of sustained effort, has been unable to advance far enough to make the amphibious operation feasible. In the third week of October, the camp is broken up, and the 28th moves eastwards to take part in the campaign officially known as Third Ypres.

The plan agreed by the Allied Armies for 1917 comprises a number of offensives on all fronts, so timed as to assist each other by depriving the enemy of the power of weakening any one of his fronts to reinforce another. Circumstances have dictated otherwise. The Russians have failed, and are in the midst of revolutionary upheaval; the Italians have been routed by the Austrians; the French have suffered enormous losses, and, together with the mutinies which follow, are rendered incapable of offensive action. The Belgians are in like mood. The burden falls more and more heavily upon the shoulders of the British Army.

While the 28th are training hard and enjoying the novel way of life that the 'Hush' Camp affords, the Third Battle of Ypres opens. By sustained attacks – at Arras, Messines, Ypres and Cambrai – Haig does indeed fulfil his fearful remit. By relentless pressure he holds the mass of German forces, enabling our Allies on other fronts to recover. The cost is high, and the particular features of the battlefield combine to give an unholy resonance to the name by which the British public come to know it: Passchendaele.

# Chapter 4

He is now in temporary command of 3 Brigade, his elevation the consequence of the Brigadier's accident. As he moves with Brigade Headquarters to the area west of Passchendaele village, he has a chance to view the countryside over which the campaign has been fought. It is utterly desolate. Scattered bricks, flung abroad by shell fire and spread untidily over the ground, are all that remains of the villages of St. Jean and Wieltje. Incessant bombardment has broken down the banks of the little water courses – the Steenbeek, Stroombeek, Lekkerboterbeek and Paddebeek – that normally drain the land. The countryside is one great mudflat, pitted with thousands of shell holes, and interspersed by wide morasses that were once rivulets. The early November sky is leaden grey. The earth is leaden grey. The soldiers who inhabit this ghost land are leaden grey, their uniforms coated with the slime that clings and works its way into every part of their daily existence. They are not fighting the Germans, they are fighting the elements, they are fighting the forces of unforgiving and unrelenting Nature.

By night, the countryside becomes alive. German Verey lights soar into the air, and soldiers curse and freeze, pausing for a moment in the work which can only be done in darkness. Units are relieved in a tortuous, laboured fashion, as incoming battalions thread their way through the slime, their progress interrupted by the passage of stretcher born wounded. Transport brings up rations, ambulance wagons warily make their way along their special trackway, guns have to be manhandled forward in absolute silence. And always there is the mud, the ubiquitous, cloying, dangerous, foul mud.

The area is only traversable by means of duckboard tracks, with rudely constructed bridges over numerous shell holes, full of water, or across the numerous streams which criss-cross the Salient. All the tracks have been marked by the German artillery, and all are shelled heavily and frequently. To leave the duck boards, for whatever reason, is to risk drowning in the shell holes. The principal track, known as Mousetrap, leads from the canal to the front line near the hamlet of Wallemolen.

In these conditions, worse than the Aubers Ridge, worse than the Somme, worse than anything that could be imagined, he has the new responsibility of taking 3 Brigade into the attack. He moves the 2nd

*Welch to take over the line — a variety of dilapidated posts and pill-boxes — opposite the Goudberg Spur, with the 28th in support, and the South Wales Borderers and Munsters in Irish Farm. His orders are to capture a part of the Goudberg Spur on 10 November.*

### 3RD (IMPERIAL) INFANTRY BRIGADE
### Account of attack carried out on 10/11/17

The intention was to seize the VAT COTTAGE RIDGE, with our Right on VOID (inclusive) and our Left at TOURNANT FARM (inclusive). The general direction of the attack was due north, timed to start at 6.15 am on 10th November.

The troops at the Acting Brigadier's disposal were:
- 1st South Wales Borderers
- 1st Gloucestershire Regt
- 2nd Bn The Welch Regiment
- 2nd Royal Munster Fusiliers
- 3rd Machine Gun Company
- 3rd Trench Mortar Battery

and guns from No 2 M.G. Coy and No 216 M.G. Coy for barrage work. The whole under the command of Lieut. Colonel A.W. Pagan, DSO, 1st Gloucestershire Regiment, in the absence of the Brigadier owing to an accident.

On the morning of the 9th the dispositions were as follows: 2nd Welch Regiment holding the line from VALOUR FARM inclusive to about v.28. central. 1st Gloucestershire Regt in support near KRONPRINZ FARM. 1st South Wales Borderers and 2nd Royal Munster Fusiliers at IRISH FARM. Brigade Headquarters at KANSAS HOUSE.

The nature of the ground over which the attack had to pass presented many difficulties...

# Chapter 4

In order to occupy the part of the ridge allotted to 3 Brigade, two groups of pill-boxes have to be captured. That on the right, roughly in a line from south to north, lies about a mile north-west of Passchendaele; that on the left, half a mile further west, is grouped around Tournant Farm. The ground to be crossed is covered in thick slime. In the centre is an impassable morass, 150 yards wide, formed by the overflowing Paddebeek stream. The left is exposed to enfilade fire from three pill-boxes situated two hundred yards north of Tournant Farm. To make matters worse, if it were possible, the weather is atrocious, with visibility reduced almost to zero.

A plan has to be made, and he does not shirk the responsibility. He makes as thorough a reconnaissance as he can, finding two vantage points from which he can see some of the ground through the driving rain. He notes one of them as a location for the Brigade Intelligence Officer. He drives his body through the mud to find the forward companies of the Welch. They are huddled in misery, their rifles the only dry things among them. Dry Welsh humour livens their conversation as they point out the possible forming up places, and the possible approaches. He realises that, after four days of living in these abominable conditions, they will certainly be unfit to attack, but can be asked to remain in the line.

He reflects deeply, calling on his accumulated store of experience of trench warfare, his knowledge of his fellow commanding officers, his feeling for what the mixture of Irish, Welsh and English can be called upon to do. He talks long and hard with the Brigade Major, with his supporting gunner, and with Moreland of the Munsters. A plan slowly evolves. It is not perfect; it is not even a good plan, because a good plan would somehow make the appalling weather lift, allowing our aeroplanes to spot, the ground dry out, the approaches clear, the slope change direction. A good plan would give him fresh troops who had not been living in these barbaric conditions, who had never been exposed to shattering shell fire, who had more than their unquenchable spirit and their dogged faith in their officers to inspire them. It is an adequate plan, the best possible in the circumstances, but it is not a good plan.

**3rd IMPERIAL INFANTRY BRIGADE**
Account of attack carried out on 10/11/17

It was decided to attack with 2 battalions, 1st South Wales Borderers on the right, and 2nd Royal Munster Fusiliers on the left. The attack on the right to form up near VALOUR FARM and to attack so that its left cleared the source of the PADDEBEEK. The attack on the left to form up near SOURCE FARM, on he right bank of the PADDEBEEK.

4 guns from No 3 M.G. Coy were detailed as Mobile Guns to each of the attacking Battalions.

It was intended to bombard with Stokes Guns the pillboxes in v.28.a but it was found impossible to mount the guns owing to the state of the ground.

The 2nd Welch Regiment were ordered to continue to hold the line and the 1st Gloucestershire Regt to remain in reserve near KRONPRINZ FARM.

The approaches to the forming up places were improved as far as was possible by the R.E. and 6th Welch Regt, and tapes were laid out at dusk on the night 9/10th instant.

The forming up was carried out without incident and without serious casualties. 2nd Royal Munster Fusiliers had considerable difficulty due to the bad going, but after an approach march of eleven hours they located TOURNANT FARM, and were in position by 4.15 am.

Report on operations on the 10th and 11th November 1917 by 1st Bn South Wales Borderers.

Battalion left IRISH FARM CAMP at 5.50 pm on the 9th Nov and proceeded up to VALOUR FARM to form up on the 'jumping off' tape. There were few casualties on the march up until the Bn reached VALOUR FARM, when A Coy lost 1 platoon all except 5 men, and B Coy had about 17 Casualties. This caused an alteration of the disposition of platoons, which took place on the tape without interference. The Bn was in position of readiness on the tape at 4.30 am, and was not molested by the enemy. From 4 am until Zero the Hun laid a fairly heavy barrage on the front line and the rear of the forward area. At Zero the Bn moved forward but before they had gone 30 yards they got amongst our own barrage which caused a number of casualties, and forced the Battalion off to the right. Our own barrage seemed very hard to follow and seemed very ragged.

# Chapter 4

Report on operations on 10th November by C.O. of 2nd Battalion Royal Munster Fusiliers

Owing to the small space available for assembly, A, C and D Coys were extremely closed up on one another. Zero attack started. A few minutes later red then green lights went up from enemy lines. A lively barrage of shells and M.G. Fire from the enemy started at Zero, laid on touching SOURCE FARM and south of it.

At 7 am I received verbal reports from runners that all objectives were carried and many prisoners were being brought in. I sent a situation report by pigeon. None of our aeroplanes were observed, but at about 7 am 2 enemy planes flew low over our lines searching them thoroughly and sending off lights. Immediately after, the enemy shortened his barrage, which was maintained till about 12 midday.

About 7.30 to 8 am I was notified that a number of men were returning from the direction of TOURNANT. I concluded that my left company was falling back. Some groups were rallied and brought back. On proceeding up the ridge I could observe the enemy counter attack. I saw 2 of our SOS signals go up some distance from me. The enemy were not very numerous, possibly a platoon extended with another following behind. They disappeared into some trenches and commenced to snipe. Before this point I could see about 150 of our men. None could fire their rifles owing to mud, and all were extremely dejected. Lieuts Mitchell and Twiss came forward with a few men, and a line was established. The Adjutant, Capt Lanktree, brought up a few more men. The remaining men halted in the area and took cover from the shelling which was very severe. The men suffered losses from the shelling and by degrees began to straggle towards the PADDEBEEK, and although several times men were brought back, by degrees the number left became very small. The men that remained were all that was left of the Battalion and were from all companies.

Capt Lanktree came to me and reported that as there were hardly any of the men left and as he could see an enemy counter attack collecting he had ordered them to withdraw across the PADDEBEEK to avoid capture. About 12 to 12.30 a company of 1st Glosters came up in support and took over the line.

**3rd IMPERIAL INFANTRY BRIGADE**
Account of attack carried out on 10th November 1917.

At 11.36 am a message from OC South Wales Borderers reported the failure to capture their objectives, but stated that he was using his reserve to clear up the situation and asking for the support of an extra company. A company of 1st Gloucestershire Regt was sent to him.

At about 12.30 pm it became clear that the 2nd Royal Munster Fusiliers had fallen back to their original lines, and at 12.45 the South Wales Borderers appeared to be falling back. At 1 pm the remainder of the Brigade Reserve were ordered to report to the South Wales Borderers but before they could come into action the Battalion was back on its original start line.

Throughout the action information reached Brigade Headquarters very slowly, mainly through the Brigade Intelligence Officer's OP (with considerable delay) or by runner message from Battalion Commanders.

*The Brigade Command Post at Kansas Cross is sited in a tiny pill-box. Although it gives welcome protection against the occasional hit by German artillery, it is cramped and inadequate. He is unused to the business of waiting for information, and the confines of this nerve centre distract him from the business of command. All his instincts demand that he be out and up with the forward troops, sharing with them the dangers and the elation of battle. But which battalion to be with?*

*The problem is that, because the Paddebeek divides the ground so effectively, he has to choose – left with the Munsters or right with the SWB? He forces himself to wait, as scraps of information come in. The first news is good: the Munsters have taken their objectives and captured numerous prisoners, a trickle of dejected Germans who pass through Brigade Headquarters. The SWB appear to have reached two of their objectives, but owing to loss of direction, appear to have been pushed eastwards, and failed to take others.*

*At 1000 the situation on the left appears to be very obscure. All telephone*

# Chapter 4

*cables have been cut by shell fire, and visibility is so bad that visual signals are ineffective. Instinct tells him that they are in trouble, and he orders a company of the 28th in Brigade Reserve to reinforce the Munsters. At 1136 an exhausted runner from the SWB reports that their objectives are still untaken. The Commanding Officer is using his own reserves, but asks for a further company from Brigade. A second company of Gloucesters is sent forward.*

*At 1138 the telephone cable connecting the Command Post with the Brigade Intelligence Officer at his forward observation post is reconnected. He reports a Munster Fusiliers Lewis gunner as saying all the Battalion's objectives have been taken. All contact is then lost, although orders come from 1 Division that the situation on the right is to be cleared up at once.*

*At 1240, 1 Division orders that Tournant farm must be retaken today. Contact is re-established with the Brigade IO.*

*'What is the situation with the Munsters?'*

*'They seem to have fallen back to their start line, Sir.'*

*'Can you see anything of the South Wales Borderers?'*

*'No Sir, but earlier I could see that they were off course. The going is absolutely awful. The FOO with me has been doing well, knocking out the enemy concentrations at v.30.a.5.8 and v.24.c.3.3, but I don't think it will do the trick.'*

*'All right, I am going to reinforce the right, and hope that they can form a defensive left flank.'*

*The Brigade Major releases the last of his reserve, the two companies of Gloucesters not yet committed. They have hardly begun their move forward when the telephone rings again.*

*'The South Wales Borderers are falling back.'*

*A message hastily scribbled on a Field Message Form is placed before him. Lieutenant Colonel Ireland and two men are the sole garrison of Source Farm.*

*'I am going forward. I want to see what the Munsters are doing. I'll go up through Wallemolen and then Mousetrap.'*

*The last man of D Company of the 28th is just ahead of him as he splashes forward. The guides from the 28th are still in place.*

*'Left after the duck board, Sir, then keep the wire on your left as far as the third shell hole.'*

*He overhears a familiar West Country voice.*

*'Good old Patsy, he'll put the fear of God up the Huns!'*

A stream of lightly wounded coming down the communication trench impedes his progress.

He slows for a stretcher case, the bearers labouring, their burden a bloody bundle under a dirty blanket. As they near Tournant Farm, D Company come under fire from the pill-boxes to the north-west. He pushes on, and finds the Munsters' Commanding Officer with D Company Commander.

'How are you going to deal with this?'

'I intend to use D Company to take both the farm, and the pill-boxes. But we need a bit of time. The trench mortars were unable to come into action, and my FOOs are all out of touch at present. As soon as we can get a fire plan sorted, they can go in.'

'Show me.'

He jumps up onto the parapet, but before anyone can follow him an airburst explodes twenty feet away. He feels the hot breath of burning lyddite, and at once a blast of pain smashes into his head. One eye is blinded, blood pours down his cheek. He falls into the trench, where the Munsters apply a first field dressing.

An orderly is arranged to escort him to the Regimental Aid Post, and within twelve hours he is at the Casualty Clearing Station.

Making allowance for every difficulty, he concludes that 3 Brigade has little reason to be proud of its deeds. His first brigade attack has been a failure.

### 3rd IMPERIAL INFANTRY BRIGADE
### Account of attack carried out on 10/11/1917

At the conclusion of the day's fighting the line ran along our original line except for Tournant Farm which then appeared to be in our hands, but was possibly mistaken for the buildings at v.29.a.0.0.

About 4.20 pm Lieutenant Colonel PAGAN was wounded while proceeding towards TOURNANT FARM to clear up the situation. Brigadier General KEMP CB arrived at Brigade Headquarters and assumed command by Divisional order at about 6 pm. This narrative has necessarily been compiled without reference to either of these officers.

# Chapter 4

This is his third wound, and the second time he has been in a Casualty Clearing Station. He notices some changes, and asks about the slit trenches, eighteen inches deep, that surround the wards.

'It's the bombers, they come over by night, and we have been hit a few times. I am sorry, the slit trenches are for the nursing sisters only, the rest of us take our chances.'

'I've got a white ticket on my wrist. What does that mean?'

'Early evacuation to England.'

'Good God, I don't need to go back to England! Two more days and I shall be as right as rain.'

'Not my decision I am afraid Colonel. The eye man reckons that there is a chance of secondary infection if it is not treated by a specialist, and that means Blighty.'

'But I can see perfectly well, it just needs dressing from time to time.'

'Sorry, orders are orders.'

Not for him they are not. He knows enough about the routine to judge the best time, and at four in the afternoon, as the night shift is due to arrive, and the ward will be full of coming and going, he puts on his dressing gown and canvas shoes. Shuffling slowly, stopping here and there to address another patient, he is at the door as a group of nurses enter. As soon as they are in, he slips through, and heads for the gate.

'Hold up there, where do you think you are going?'

'Colonel Pagan, inspecting the outside lines. When did you come on duty?'

'Ten this morning, why?'

'You should have been told. It's a Code Red Alert. Any suspicious movement has to be checked. You stay at your post while I check the perimeter.'

The sentry returns to his hut, mumbling about 'Bleeding Orders, Bleeding Officers, Bleeding Nutters, roll on death, the end of the war's too far way...'

The CCS is on the main road up to the front. He knows that as soon as darkness approaches lorries will begin their nightly resupply runs. He waits until he sees one approaching with the distinctive red numeral One of his division, and moves into the road.

'Cor, it's Colonel Pagan. You don't want to be out in those clothes. Here, Sir, take this poshteen, it'll warm you.'

'Thank you, Corporal, you must have done time in the Shiny.'

'I did, Sir, with the 28th, but before your time. I was medically downgraded after Mons, but I managed to wangle a job with the ASC. So I see the lads quite often – what's left of them. I know all about you though, Sir, they are always talking about you. I'll get you to the Divisional Dump, but then I'll have to leave you. Your own Battalion transport can pick you up there. What a story though, eh? Colonel Pagan in a dressing gown!'

By the time they arrive at the Divisional Dump, darkness has fallen. At the entrance, a Military Policeman is checking each vehicle as it comes in. His bright bull's eye exposes the unusual attire of the driver's mate.

'What's this, a lunatic? Who have you got here, Corporal?'

'Colonel Pagan, Commanding Officer of the 1st Battalion the Gloucestershire Regiment,' announces the driver, with all the grandeur of a Royal levee.

'And what might Colonel Pagan of the Gloucestershire Regiment be doing riding in your cab in a dressing gown?'

'Look here Corporal, I had better explain. I have been summoned urgently by the General. I was on a spot of local leave, and had to depart in a bit of a hurry. The fact is a young lady now owns my uniform.'

'If you wouldn't mind waiting a moment, Sir, I had better check with the DAPM.'

As soon as the redcap's back is turned, he is out of the cab and moving off towards the 3 Brigade bay. He passes an ASC officer and greets him with a cheery wave. Just then, the Deputy Assistant Provost Marshal arrives, to see a short, balding man in a dressing gown acting in a most familiar way with an officer.

The DAPM demands his pay-book, and the story is repeated. The evening is drawing on, there are a hundred matters pressing for attention, and when the bald-headed man spots his RQMS in the distance, and is instantly recognised, the inquisition is over.

And a regimental legend is born.

'Colonel, could I see you for a moment?'

'Come in Doc, what is it?'

'It's all a bit embarrassing. You see I have just received an extraordinary note from the ADMS at Division. It says that Lieutenant Colonel Pagan is posted as an absentee from no 10 CCS. The ADMS has added, in his own handwriting, that no further treatment by Army Medical Services is permitted for him as he has defied medical advice.'

# Chapter 4

'And does the Assistant Director of Medical Services suggest how I should continue treatment for my eye – which, by the way, is healing extremely well under your attention?'

'The thing is, Colonel, do you think you could not mention that I have been treating you? It would mean a fearful row if it got out.'

'I'll offer you a deal. You find me a local Frenchie who can look at it once a day, and Mum's the word on my part.'

'All right Colonel, but Mum's the word.'

On the day that 3 Brigade are repulsed at the Goudberg Spur, the offensive is called off. The 28th move to a series of comfortable camps, and leave is regular. Men get home every six months, although the leave trains have smashed windows, which make for chilly journeys. Life in the camps is agreeable, and at night everyone turns out to watch the cat and mouse game between the enemy bombers and our searchlights and anti-aircraft guns. Rarely is a hit observed.

The 1st Division now holds the line south of the Houthulst Forest. Here the main Dixmude-Ypres road crosses the Yser Canal, and it is south again of this point that the 28th take over the line. Two of the companies are protected by battered pill-boxes, remnants of the old German line. They are inches deep in water. Battalion Headquarters is in a pill-box so tiny that no one can move without knocking something over. If the door is shut, the inhabitants suffocate; if it is open they freeze.

The ground has endured terrific shelling by both sides, as a result of which the banks of the streams that traverse it have been destroyed. The result is a huge swamp. Some 500 yards behind the Outpost Line, the main line of resistance is marginally more comfortable, but there is constant activity as the enemy's lines are probed.

**3rd INFANTRY BRIGADE, INTELLIGENCE SUMMARY 14th DEC 1917**

A Company from 1st Gloucesters under the command of Captain Smith left our line at 7.30 pm 13th instant, for the purpose of locating the enemy line and, if possible, to establish enemy identification. After leaving our line at u.4.a.o.o they found a road which ran rather more to the North than the bearing taken previously taken had indicated. As no other road could be found the patrol followed this one for about 400 yards, where a large timber shelter was reached. This was searched, but nothing was found in it, and it had no sign of recent occupation. On advancing a further 50 yards the road came to an end and a further 100 yards from here the road became impassable through water. At this point there was a row of stunted trees on the left. A piece of timber was placed in the branches of one tree and it is hoped to identify this in daylight.

The night was exceedingly dark and progress was very slow. The patrol returned at 12.15 am.

Whilst reconnoitring, the patrol commander saw 3 enemy leave the pillbox at u.4.a.64.25. A little later a party of 30 Germans visited this pillbox and two others and apparently carried out a relief.

The 28th is happy to come out of the line on 21 December, and to celebrate Christmas, for once on the 25th itself. Again, every kind of good thing has been sent from home, together with money to buy turkeys and beer. It is the Battalion's fourth Christmas on the Western Front, and the prospects for any end to the fighting seem remote. However, events elsewhere are shaping the fate of the British Army in France.

As the new year dawns throughout Europe and Asia, war weariness is setting in, nowhere more so than in Germany. Food shortages, exacerbated by the Allied blockade, are the pretext for strikes and social unrest. Disturbances are so serious that troops have to be called out to deal with them. The General Staff, dominated by Ludendorff, are well aware that a protracted war means for them a lost war. As Haig has been predicting since the war began, it is the side which hangs on longest which will prevail.

# Chapter 4

However, amid the gloom, there is for Germany a strong ray of light. Their brilliant strategic coup of moving Lenin through Europe to burst like a thunderclap upon a Russia already in the throes of a nascent revolution has produced the effect they have dreamed of. For the High Command, the Russian collapse means the early prospect of heaven-sent reinforcement; a breakthrough on the Western Front – for the Germans agree with Haig and Robertson that this is the 'centre of gravity' of the war – could decide the war in a matter of weeks. They can also expect rich pickings: the treaty of Brest-Litovsk enforces on Russia the loss to Germany of thirty-two per cent of her agricultural land, fifty-four per cent of her industry and eighty-nine per cent of her coal. The writing is on the wall for the Allies should they be forced to make peace on German terms.

The French are in a questionable state. The mutinies of the previous year have been followed by a very careful and gentle easing of conditions for the poilus, under the nursing of their new commander-in-chief, Petain. They are willing to resume the fight, but their quality and endurance are unknown quantities.

The British Army is in turmoil. Lloyd-George, an unrepentant opponent of the 'Westerners', scores three blows against his own commander-in-chief in the field. He engineers the downfall of Robertson, Haig's constant supporter as CIGS, and several major members of GHQ in France; he foists an uncomfortable chain of command on the BEF, so that uncertainty and divided counsels cloud command and control; and most damagingly he reduces the number of infantry available to Haig, just as the Germans are building an advantage in manpower. All this results in reorganisation and confusion even as the British are forced to take over an additional forty miles of front from the French. While 141 battalions disappear from the BEF's order of battle, while each brigade loses one of its four infantry units, and each division loses a brigade, at the same time wholesale realignment of the Army is taking place, under strange leaders.

The German build-up in the west has been under way since November, when there are 150 divisions. By early February the number rises to 174. It will eventually peak at 200.

For 3 Brigade, the reorganisation involves the removal of the Royal Munster Fusiliers, transferred to the 16th Division, and the disbandment of the 10th Gloucesters. The disappearance of their sister battalion is saddening, but the 28th benefit by gaining 100 good men. Their prime task for the next few weeks is to strengthen the defences that will be required to hold the German offensive that is expected. The line is known as the Army Line, and the portion on which the 28th is employed bristles with concrete emplacements. The continuous trenches are more like concrete walls, raised above the ground with foundations below the surface, and huge underground dugouts.

Patrolling is a constant occupation, and Captain Smith MC, Commander of C Company, sets a standard that is hard to beat. Younger officers strive to emulate his deeds.

### PATROL REPORTS

7/1/18. 2 Lt GA WILSON & 8 OR. To discover the whereabouts of the enemy, what he is doing, and if possible obtain a prisoner. Patrol left our line at u.3.b.2.4 and proceeded to u.3.b.2.7 and then u.3.b.65.85. Nothing was seen or heard of the enemy.

(After the conclusion of this patrol, a congratulatory message from the Brigade Commander is read out to all officers of the 28th.)

7/1/18. 2 Lt GFM FORBES and 8 OR. To discover the enemy, what he is doing, and if possible obtain a prisoner. Patrol left our line at u.4.c.7.7 and proceeded along North side of road for about 120 yards. Shouting was heard from the direction of SURCOUFF FARM.

7/1/18. 2 Lt WM DAVIES and 9 OR. Discover the nature of hostile works reported in course of construction south of X Roads at u.5.a.57.90. The patrol left our line and proceeded in a northerly direction just East of the PANAMA HOUSE-RENARD FARM Road. They found an enemy post at u.5.a.85.75 occupied and heard talking and whistling in the direction of the X Roads. Owing to the extreme darkness the patrol was unable to confirm the nature of the defensive works, but ascertained that there was no wire in front of the post.

# Chapter 4

### 3rd INFANTRY BRIGADE HANDING OVER NOTES 14/1/18

<u>Enemy Activity</u>. It would appear that the enemy is establishing a line of strong points, RENARD Fm, SURCOUFF, KASBAH, and is connecting them up by strong wire. There are no signs of enemy trenches on the whole front, the enemy is very passive, and no patrols have been met with.

<u>Our Lines.</u> Barbed wire, interlaced nightly, before Outpost Line. A little barbed wire, interlaced nightly, along Main Line of Resistance. Shelters have been built, and 60 men can be accommodated.

<u>Work on hand to be continued.</u> First line of wire along 2nd line of posts. Making bullet-proof the battle positions in the Main Line of Defence. Replacing of duck board tracks forward of Btn H'qrs of Battalions in the Line.

<u>Suggested Work.</u> Improvement of accommodation. Interlacing of loose barbed wire along Main Line of Resistance. 2nd line of concertina wire along 2nd line of posts.

### 3rd INFANTRY BRIGADE DEFENCE SCHEME 18/2/18

The Brigade is disposed as follows:

| | |
|---|---|
| Brigade Headquarters | HOSPITAL FARM |
| 1st S.Wales Bord. | do. |
| 1st Glouc R. | CARDOEN FARM |
| 2nd Welch R. | SIEGE CAMP |
| No 3 MG Coy | do. |
| 3rd TM Batty | do. |

In the event of a hostile attack, the Brigade will probably be required to defend the 'BATTLE ZONE' on the frontage of the 1st Division.

The Battle Zone Main Defensive Line includes the following defended localities:
MOUSE TRAP FARM

**JULIET FARM**
**OBLONG FARM**
**RACECOURSE FARM**
**BOCHE CASTEL**
**MINTY FARM**

**The Outpost Line of the Main Battle Zone runs through the following points:**
**VANHEULE FARM**
**CORNER COT**
**ALBERTA**
**REGINA CROSS**
**FERDINAND FARM**

**On receipt of the order 'STAND TO' all units in the Brigade will hold themselves in readiness to move at 15 minutes notice.**

**On the order to 'MOVE', 500 men per battalion, with their Lewis Guns will move to Railway at HOSPITAL TRAIN and entrain at ZERO plus two hours, and detrain at St JEAN at ZERO plus 2½ hours. Zero will be the time at which the order is sent out. The remainder of battalions, Trench Mortar Battery and Machine Gun Company will move at the same time and march forward via DAWSONS CORNER.**

**The Battle Zone will be defended as follows:**
**Left Sector:**     2nd Welch Regt
**Centre Sector:**  1st Gloucester Regt.
**Right Sector:**   1st S.Wales Borderers.

The loss of the fourth battalion is felt acutely. The position will lack the depth that a good defensive position requires. Other orders follow on 22 February, which outline the new concept on which the British Army will attempt with its weakened fifty-nine divisions to confront the eighty-one divisions which the Germans are building up against it. Each divisional sector is divided into three zones. The first is the Front System of the Forward Zone, containing the Outpost Line, commanded by the Brigade in the Line at the time of the attack.

The second is the Support System of the Forward Zone, under command of the Support Brigade. This will consist of a framework of strong points, each normally adapted for one or two machine guns and an infantry platoon. This framework forms a system of organised defensive localities, so sited as to form, with their garrisons, a skeleton to assist the Brigade in Support in an active defence of their Zone. The permanent infantry garrisons of these posts will be found by one company in each Battalion Sector.

The Battle Zone comes under command of the Reserve Brigade. It will move to a 'jumping off' position, from which it can give support as required.

## SUPPORT BRIGADE DEFENCE SCHEME

It is conceivable that owing to the threat of a hostile offensive, it might become necessary for the Support System of the Forward Zone to be occupied so that the troops will be on the spot for occupying their fire positions at a moment's notice. Such a state of affairs might last for 48 hours or even longer. Under such circumstances the permanent localities organised would continue to be manned. Units will move from their present billets to the positions indicated on receipt of the message from Brigade Headquarters 'Battle Positions.'

Throughout late February and into March, little activity by the Germans in their positions opposite the 28th is visible. However, there is a good deal of shelling during the day, and frequent aerial dog fights. On one occasion a British aeroplane is shot down; its pilot is unhurt.

On 4 March the 28th take over the Poelcappelle position, with Meunier House on the right. The village retains its outline form, but massive concrete works give it an impression of great strength. On the morning of 7 March the Germans try to raid Meunier House. A quick but heavy barrage is put down, and then the infantry advance. The Gloucesters are busy working on the wire defences, and suffer several casualties from the bombardment, but the remainder occupy their trenches and drive the enemy off.

On the 8th the Battalion is relieved, and prepares for a raid that has been ordered for 13 March. Divisional headquarters desperately needs to identify its German opposition.

*The raid is to be on two enemy posts near Cameron House, with the intention of bringing back a prisoner for intelligence purposes. Orders have been issued by Brigade Headquarters, and as he reads them, he gives a sigh of amused exasperation. They are very comprehensive orders, giving minute instructions on how documents are to be searched for, the exact number of officers and men in the raiding party, its assembly area, and the covering artillery fire. It even details the synchronisation of watches, by means of sending one to the gunners, and the same watch later to the Gloucesters.*

*The same, or better, orders could have been put together by the commander of B Company, which is to conduct the raid. A simple mission could have been given: 'You are to bring back a prisoner from Cameron House', and the rest would follow. The 'over command' he muses, is the result of the lack of training in other parts of the Army – most notably in the New Army divisions, where such detailed instruction from on high is necessary.*

*He moves up Dimple Trench, and over to Von Tirpitz farm, the location of B Company headquarters. There he picks up Captain Mallet, and the two of them move off with the key NCOs who are to conduct the raid. They slog over to Wallemolen, from where Cameron House can best be viewed. He returns to B Company Headquarters with them, confident that they are as well prepared as it is possible to be for a very tricky operation.*

*As he settles to a mess tin of warm stew, a runner arrives from Battalion Headquarters. His news is greeted with enthusiasm. The indefatigable Captain Smith, patrolling expert extraordinary, has been out that evening with a patrol from C Company. Their mission is to identify a German earthwork on the Westroosebeke road. Guile, fieldcraft and luck combine to reward their courage. A German sergeant-major and three men happen to be taking the night air as they approach. A rush, a quick struggle, and they are captives. The raid by B Company is cancelled.*

# Chapter 4

At five minutes past five on the morning of 21 March – 117 years to the day since the 28th won the Back Badge at Alexandria – the Germans commence their bombardment of the fourteen divisions of General Gough's Fifth Army, thinly spread over forty-two miles of front. Across the whole front of the offensive – the 'Kaiserschlacht' – which includes three diversionary sectors, six and a half thousand guns and three and a half thousand trench mortars produce a devastating effect. In many places the entire defending force in the Forward and Battle Zones disappears.

Five hours after the opening of the bombardment, the German infantry come over, assisted by an all-encompassing fog. Great gaps are torn in the British line, which could be exploited by cavalry. Fortunately for the British the Germans have none, and their exploitation is limited to the speed of their infantry on foot.

The 28th are initially not affected.

**War Diary (1918) of 1st Battalion the Gloucestershire Regiment (28th)**

**22-3-18. D Company relieved A Company in the Support System of the Forward Zone. Remainder of Battalion training.**

**22-3-18. Battalion training.**

**24-3-18. Church Parade and bathing. Working parties. Lieut Col AW Pagan DSO left Battalion to command 184th Inf Bde.**

*'The Divisional Commander is here to see you, Colonel.'*

*'Good morning, General, what brings you to the 28th?'*

*Major General Strickland hesitates. A ferocious perfectionist, he is highly respected in the Regiment for his professional ability and his interest in the soldiers' welfare. His bristling manner hides a deep human sympathy.*

*'Quite a lot, actually, Patsy. Any chance of a snifter?'*

'Ration rum?'

'Perfect. First I need to bring you up to date on the Hun offensive. We all knew it was coming, but we had not expected things to be quite this bad. First Army is holding out pretty well, but don't spread it about, Fifth Army has taken a heavy pasting, and it looks as if the Hun intend to push through at St Quentin and take Amiens. You may well look surprised. I'm afraid some people are getting pretty rattled, and one or two are not quite up to the mark. Which brings me to the purpose of my visit. Its good news and bad news. First, the bad news. I am afraid you are for off. You don't need to tell me that you don't want to go; I know that. I don't want you to go either. There is no question that we will be for the high jump pretty soon, it's just a matter of time before the Hun turns his attention on us. We will need all the good men we can muster, and you are one of my best. In fact, between ourselves, I fought like hell to hang on to you. The good news is that you are to get a brigade. It's 184, South Midland Brigade, good Territorials. Something to cheer you up: the 2/5th Gloucesters are in it, so you'll have some of your own Regiment around.'

'Where are they, and when do I report?'

'They are in Colin Mackenzie's 61st Division, Fifth Army, so God knows where they are at present. Last heard of, they were just west of St Quentin. You are to get there as soon as possible, the Brigade Commander has been wounded, and the situation looks a bit sticky. So you have little time to say your goodbyes, and hand over to Gould. But Tweedie is on his way, he should be here in a day or two.'

'Good Lord, I find it hard to take it all in. Could I possibly have a car and driver from the Staff Pool?'

'Of course, he can fit you and Nicholls in comfortably.'

# Chapter 5

*It feels queer at first – the red tabs, thoughtfully donated by the Brigade Commander, the crown and three pips, the car – but the journey from the north to the south of the British sector gives him space to put his thoughts in order. To leave the Regiment at this crucial time, when it could be facing fearful odds, is the hardest thing he has had to endure in his forty years. His mind is full of the hurried farewells, the men pressing to shake his hand, to wish him God Speed, to tell him, in their inarticulate fashion, how much he means to them. One wag even shouts 'Come back soon!' But he knows there is no return, at least while this beastly war is on. Perhaps, if peace ever comes, he can again declare himself the King of Kings, the Emperor of Emperors, the Commanding Officer of the 28th! But not now. Now he has greater responsibilities.*

*The first leg takes them to Bethune, and a chance to catch news from a harassed staff officer, who tells him that he knows for a fact that nothing exists of Fifth Army's Outpost Line, and heavy fighting is also affecting part of Third Army.*

*At Arras, the news is even grimmer: Fifth Army is in tatters, Amiens is in danger. At Albert, while they fill up at an ASC fuel dump, he begins to sense the air of uncertainty that seems to affect everyone from senior to junior. Men lower their voices as they exchange rumours, they glance occasionally over their shoulder, they break off abruptly from conversation when they see red tabs.*

*They press on, and he spells the driver at the wheel. It may not be etiquette, it may even be against regulations, but he needs to get on. Thirty hours have passed since he left the Ypres sector, and as they approach Amiens he hears the roar of artillery. They pass the cathedral, its roof showing the effects of the German long range artillery which is already in range. A military policeman warns them that the Hun is in Harbonnières, and advises that they leave on the road through Corbie.*

*The signs of a retreat are all about them. Wounded and stragglers pass them, their faces bearing the haggard look of men who have reached the limit of endurance. The traffic is an eloquent intermingling of troops, guns and civilians evacuating as much of their property as possible upon wagons and carts, which are piled high with children, tables, utensils, bedsteads, farm implements and mattresses. Artillery batteries just off the road are firing desperately, sappers stand by every bridge and culvert ready to blow them when the order is given.*

*At Corbie, they pull in to the Reinforcement Camp to see a strange sight. Some 600 men are on parade, but from what unit? There are Fusiliers, Borderers, Light Infantry and Ulstermen. There are ASC drivers without lorries, and gunners without guns. There are supply clerks. There are cooks and bath operators. There are some twenty officers, as varied in provenance as the men. A more senior officer is arguing with the Officer Commanding the camp.*

*'Good morning, I am Brigadier Pagan, General Officer Commanding 184 Brigade. Do you mind telling me what the devil is going on here?'*

*'Little, Sir, Fifth Borderers. I was on leave when I saw the name Hargicourt in one of the rags, so I knew my battalion was involved. I got to Folkestone p.d.q, had to wait for the fog to clear, got the first boat, trained, lorry hopped, walked until I got here. I have prised 600 men from the Camp Comedian here, and I was just arguing for more when you arrived Sir.'*

*'And what are you proposing to do with this 600?'*

*'Reinforce my regiment, Sir.'*

*'Good luck, Little, if everyone shows the sort of pluck you have done, we don't have too much to worry about.'*

*At Villers-Brettoneux they see yet more extraordinary sights. Another group of stray men, this time under a red tabbed staff captain. He is from Hunter's Brigade, and has collected the brigade signal staff, remnants of the Sapper Field Companies, and some stray men of the 66th Division. They are forming fours even as shells begin to drop around them, hurling bricks and mortar, tiles, slates and timber in all directions. A few yards from them lie two dead men and three dead horses, and on the church steps, drooping and alone, sits a little old withered nun. She will not leave, despite the entreaties of the soldiers. She does not look up when the brigade staff and their oddments swing by on their way to battle, singing 'Goodbyee, goodbyee, there's a silver lining in the skyee.' A shell bursts just as they leave the square, dressed in all sorts of kit, just as they have left their work. Cooks' sons and dukes' sons; clerks in spectacles; sappers, signalling officers, staff officers with red tabs, men who clean saucepans. They swing away eastward, towards the roar of battle. Soon they are out of sight, but every now and then, between the reverberating shell*

# Chapter 5

*explosions, a few words of their song can be heard. 'Goodbyee ... Skyee...' And still the little old nun does not move.*

At 184 Brigade Headquarters, Howitt, the Brigade Major, gaunt and moustachioed, shows signs of the strain of the past week, but his voice is calm and even as he rapidly outlines the brigade's precarious position.

'We were around Holnon Wood in the Battle Zone when the show kicked off. Five hours of really heavy bombardment which did for most of the Outpost Line, but also hit rear areas. It was mixed with gas, and with the fog that was so thick you could hardly see your hand in front of your face, the Hun was soon all over our chaps. All telephone cables were cut, and we had little idea of what was what until the first runners came through. The Oxfords lost pretty heavily, I am afraid. We have been on the move ever since, first to Billancourt, then Languevoisin, then to hold the bridgehead at Quesnoy. On the 25th Colonel Wetherall, who was in temporary command after Brigadier Hill had been wounded, was himself hit by shell splinters.'

He nods, he has already heard the story of how Howitt held the arteries of his shattered neck together, saving his life.

'Who has been commanding since?'

'Another Gloucester, Colonel Lawson of the 2/5th. That day we had some assistance from two companies of French. We moved again, each time a little further back, first to Mezières, then to Le Quesnel, then to Hailles. This morning we arrived at Marcelcave, and we had hardly got into some sort of position when we received orders that we are to attack Warfuse and Lamotte, in conjunction with 183 Brigade. So Colonel Lawson is at the Brigade OP which we have set up with the gunners here.' He indicates on the map spread before them. 'He is giving out orders at the moment.'

'What shape is the Brigade in?'

'The Oxfords are down to about 200, the Gloucesters and the Berkshires about 300 each. They are dog tired, they are hungry and thirsty – although the supply system has worked wonders, it just can not keep up. The Berkshires were down a bit when their CO was killed – not many battalions have a VC commanding them – but they are rallying, the Oxfords of course have been the worst affected, and the Gloucesters are – well, you know what Gloucesters are like – they don't say much, but they are steady as a rock. The main problem is lack of sleep. Take them all out of the line for twenty four hours, two days if

possible, and let them sleep. They will be right as rain after.'
   *'I'll go forward and watch the attack. How do I get to the OP?'*
   *'Hunter, the Staff Captain, will take you up.'*

The men are brought up in buses. These jaded soldiers, dog tired, battle stained and exhausted in body and spirit are to carry out the southern part of the assault, while cavalry attack from the west. The Brigade has less than eight hundred rifles left, and not a man is in a fit condition to undergo this fiery ordeal. Yet one and all behave with the greatest gallantry, advancing across flat, open grassland with no cover, and without artillery support.

**WAR DIARY OF 184th INFANTRY BRIGADE (1918)**

28-3-18. Orders were received that the brigade was to attack WARFUSEE and LAMOTTE at 11 am, in conjunction with 183 Inf Bde on its left.

Brig. Gen A.W. Pagan DSO took over command of the Brigade.
At 12 am the attack moved forward in extended line and immediately came under heavy MG fire from WARFUSEE and LAMOTTE to its front, and from BAYONVILLERS to its right flank. The artillery was unable to deal with the MGs and after heavy casualties the attack had to withdraw when within 200 yards of its objective.

At 6 pm the enemy attacked and WIENCOURT having been evacuated, he secured a footing along the railway on the right of the Brigade, causing a general withdrawal. A line was next established about 500 yards W of MARCELCAVE running approximately North to South.

Dispositions of the Brigade were as follows:

| | |
|---|---|
| 184 Bde HQ | in the Railway Cutting |
| 2/5 GLOSTERS | North of the Railway |
| 2/4 R.BERKS | Astride the Railway |
| 2/4 OXFORDS | South of the Railway |

# Chapter 5

*He watches from his vantage point as the men stream back; no panic retreat this, but an ordered withdrawal. Junior officers throw out defensive flanks, form rear guards, and handle the action with a skill which he finds encouraging. Terriers they may be, but two years of war have hardened 184 Brigade into a professional force he can be proud of.*

*German aeroplanes aid the attack. They fly low, and the putt-putt-putt of their machine guns confirms the many targets they find among the moving infantry and the gun lines. In the flaring twilight, noisy with explosions, he can see the Germans advancing in full strength, wave after wave, column after column. Wherever he looks he sees an inferno of burning villages, stores flaring, ammunition dumps detonating. He sees the ambulances trying to evacuate the many wounded, he sees the fugitives crowding the roads. It is a scene such as Breughel might have conjured.*

*'Time to go, Sir.' It is the gunner FOO, so fresh faced he seems to belong in school, not to be a participant in this horrific scene.*

*'Time to go,' he agrees.*

Throughout the 29th the enemy contents himself with registering his artillery on the Brigade's trenches, and builds up his strength in Marcelclave. While the battered battalions catch their breath, Brigade Headquarters moves to the eastern outskirts of Villers-Brettoneux.

On the 30th, the enemy attacks, and the Brigade's right flank, manned by the desperately weak Oxfords, is driven in from Abercourt northwards. The Gloucesters are hard pressed north of the railway, and give ground for an hour before a final effort from exhausted men turns the Germans out of their line. The Germans then move forward under a heavy barrage, to occupy a line 400 yards from the Brigade front line.

An Australian brigade counter attacks and regains some of the lost ground. At 1000 the eagerly awaited order is received that the Brigade is to be relieved by an Australian battalion, and will move in reserve to Gentelles, south of the Amiens road. On the 31st the relief is completed, and the Brigade can relax, but for a short time only. On 2 April, they move again to billets based on Tailly.

# Gloucestershire Hero

Casualties since the opening of the German offensive on 21 March are:

| | |
|---|---|
| Brigade Headquarters | one officer and four ORs |
| Gloucesters | twenty officers and 500 ORs |
| Oxfords | twenty-three officers and 700 ORs |
| Berkshires | twenty officers and 500 ORs |

The Brigade can muster the strength of a battalion.

*Now is his first opportunity to get around the Brigade. He ensures that he sees every man. No formal inspection this; he moves informally from billet to billet, chatting and joking, hearing the tales from the shattering experience they have undergone. He is satisfied with what he sees. Howitt is right. A day or two of rest, a chance to wash and shave, to eat a hot meal, to sleep an unbroken sleep, to be away from the ear splitting noise of the artillery, to be out of danger — these are the tonic these men need.*

*At Tailly he is with the battalion headquarters of the Oxfords when shouts of surprise and joy erupt.*

*'What's going on?'*

*'It's Bennett.'*

*'Impossible, he was taken at Marcelclave.'*

*'It's me all right, turned up like a bad penny!'*

*'How do you do — I'm Pagan, your new Brigadier. I heard that you had been captured, and Robinson is now in command. Tell us your story.'*

*'I decided to visit a platoon near the railway bridge, but ran straight in to the Hun. They pushed me back to their Regimental Headquarters, and I was kept there for twenty four hours. I was surprised that they made no attempt to interrogate me, and they then sent me back to Harbonnières, where they had put up a very sloppy sort of cage. They still treated me decently, but I had nothing to eat for two days. The fact was, they are themselves terribly short of rations. The guards on the cage were constantly hungry, and all they seemed to talk about was food. They apologised for not feeding us, but said that they just had nothing. I got jolly depressed about this I can tell you, and Blake of the Warwicks and I decided to have a go at getting out. It was not too hard. We waited until dark and then slipped under the wire, ran for cover, and then wandered around until we found a house just off the main square which*

*seemed to be abandoned. We found bread and cheese, a bottle or two of wine and some raw vegetables. We fell on them, I can tell you. We tiptoed upstairs, and hid in a cupboard for the night.*

*'Now, here's the rum part. Next morning we crept out of the cupboard at dawn, and peeped out of the window towards the square. We began to see curious sights. Strange figures, who looked little like soldiers, and certainly were not heading towards Amiens, were making their way in the opposite direction. There were men driving cows before them; others who carried a hen under one arm and a box of note-paper under the other. Men who had torn a silk drawing room curtain off its rod and were dragging it to the rear. Men with writing paper and coloured notebooks. Men dressed up in comic disguise. One had a top hat on his head. Men who were so drunk they could hardly walk. The odd thing was their officers seemed to have no control over them. We tend to think of discipline in the Hun Army as ferocious, but I can tell you, there was no discipline in this lot.*

*Well, to cut a long story short, we stayed in that house for another day, then slipped out at night, and cut across country until we were up with the German line. We lay up for another day, then ran like hell and somehow got through.'*

'Our advance became slower and slower. The hopes and wishes which had soared beyond Amiens had to be recalled. Facts must be treated as facts..., we ought to have shouted in the ear of every single man, "Press on to Amiens. Put in your last ounce. Perhaps Amiens means decisive victory. Capture Villers-Brettoneux whatever happens, so that from its heights we can command Amiens with masses of our heavy artillery." It was in vain. Our strength was exhausted.'

Field Marshal von Hindenburg

Now begins a period of reinforcement, re-equipping and retraining. Drafts of men come from the most surprising sources: cooks, shoemakers, tailors, postmen, mess orderlies and transport men – soldiers who have, perhaps some years before, received basic training, but who have since lived a very different life to that of their new comrades of 184 Brigade. Huge quantities of new equipment are required, and huge quantities are provided, from entrenching tools to Lewis guns, from boots to cookers. The speed with which Ordnance provides these supplies meets with universal praise.

Most fortunate are the Oxfords – the 2/4th Battalion Oxfordshire and Buckingham Light Infantry. The 2/1st Bucks Battalion of the regiment formed the fourth battalion of the Brigade until the reduction of infantry establishments early in the New Year. Retitled the 25th Entrenching Battalion, and employed on building the Army Line, they have been caught up in the fighting around Nesle. On their own initiative, they avail themselves of the general confusion to march, without authority, to Avesne. Here they meet up with the 2/4th and add 300 good men to their strength. Soon after comes a draft of 430 from England. Many are boys, but among them are veterans who are worth their weight in gold.

Intensive training of specialists is undertaken. Riflemen become Lewis gunners, bombers become signallers, private soldiers become non-commissioned officers, and are instructed in their duties by regimental sergeant majors and company sergeant majors. Junior officers take command of companies; more senior officers, second in command or commanding officer. The fighting has taken a heavy toll of commanders.

The new Brigade commander is everywhere. An officer of the 2/5th Gloucesters sums up the general opinion. 'He is a born fighter with the heart of a lion. He seems to have two absorbing interests in life – the Gloucestershire Regiment and Rugby Football.'

On 11 April, the Brigade entrains for the north. The intention is to move the brigade to a quiet sector at Laventie, in the old Ypres Salient. But it is on this day that the Germans switch the direction of their offensive, and break through on the Lys, south of Armentières. There will be no rest for 184 Brigade.

**SPECIAL ORDER OF THE DAY**

**By Field Marshal Sir Douglas Haig, Commander-in-Chief, British Armies in France**

**TO ALL RANKS OF THE BRITISH ARMY IN FRANCE AND FLANDERS**

# Chapter 5

Three weeks ago today the enemy began his terrific attacks against us on a fifty-mile front. His objects are to separate us from the French, to take the Channel Ports and destroy the British Army.

In spite of already throwing 106 divisions into the battle and enduring the most reckless sacrifice of human life, he has as yet made little progress towards his goals.

We owe this to the determined fighting and self-sacrifice of our troops. Words fail me to express the admiration which I feel for the splendid resistance offered by all ranks of our Army under the most trying circumstances.

Many amongst us are now tired. To those I would say that Victory will belong to the side which holds out the longest. The French Army is moving rapidly and in great force to our support.

There is no other course open to us but to fight it out. Every position must be held to the last man: there must be no retirement. With our backs to the wall and believing in the justice of our cause each one of us must fight on to the end. The safety of our homes and the Freedom of mankind alike depend upon the conduct of each one of at this critical time.

**General Headquarters**                    **Tuesday 11th April 1918**

*The first signs of impending trouble come at Hangest, north of Amiens, where the Brigade entrains. He reads the day's Continental Daily Mail with quickening excitement, and a brief conversation with an excited Rail Transport Officer, while the soldiers wait for the order to fill the train, confirms what lies ahead. He consults the map with Howitt.*

*'We detrain here, at Steenbecque, just north of St Venant. It looks as if we should take advantage of the Nieppe Forest to concentrate, while I get orders from Division.'*

*The night is overcast, which saves the trains from the attention of enemy aeroplanes. The journey through St Pol, Chocques and Lillers is a succession of halts. The skyline is lit occasionally by the glare of mines and munitions factories, the air rent by the booming of artillery, and the sleep of the soldiers by the grinding of brakes.*

A staff car at Steenbecque whisks him to Isbergues. The road is packed with refugees, and he experiences a strong sense of deja vu: this is the scene he saw just two weeks before at Amiens. An excited staff officer south of Thiennes tells him that the enemy is in Robecq, and already crossing the La Bassée canal. He decides to await a clearer report. At a very reduced Divisonal headquarters General Colin Mackenzie, solid, unruffled, jovial, briefs him.

'The situation is a complete mess. The two Portuguese divisions holding the front at Merville have legged it, the 51st Division tried to plug the gap and has been cut to pieces, and we are the only thing between the Hun and the Channel. Now, I want you to bring 184 Brigade to the right of the Warwicks. You will have your left on Calonne, and your right on Robecq. Give yourself what depth you can, but I cannot guarantee you any gunner support for now. If you can find a helpful battery commander, hang on to him for dear life. One last thing.' He lowers his voice. 'The C-in-C has called for every position to be held to the last man. There can be no withdrawal. We hold the Hun here or it's the end of the war. I know I can rely on you, Pagan. Good luck. Mountfield here will give you a marked map – God knows how accurate it is.'

His mind clears. There can be no withdrawal. The future of the war, the freedom of England, depend on him and his brigade.

On the edge of the Nieppe Forest, as dawn is breaking, he briefs Howitt, whose lean face betrays no emotion as he hears the account of muddle and confusion.

'We'll put the Oxfords on the left, the Berkshires on the right, and the Gloucesters in depth, here, here and here. Make out the orders and brief the COs. I'm going forward to Mont Bernanchon. Perhaps I can get a sense of the battle from there. We will put Brigade Headquarters in St Venant. I will meet you there at midday. Nicholls, come on, we're off.'

A he enters St Venant on his way through to the south, he is startled to hear the sound of small arms fire. Surely the Hun cannot be here already? It is in fact the work of someone anticipating the worst, and as he passes Robecq cemetery he watches the blaze of exploding shells from a dump which some over excited officer has decided to destroy. An acre of explosives is on fire.

From his vantage point he can see that the hardest fighting is to the north east. Merville and Calonne are almost blotted out in smoke, and the air is thronged with aeroplanes. The countryside is pleasantly rural, and the orchards and farms will provide excellent cover and strong points for his brigade.

He moves back to St Venant, well satisfied. He has chosen his ground.

The Brigade moves into position none too soon. The Oxfords have a sharp fight with some adventurous Germans who have outstripped their comrades on the left flank. They take some thirty casualties around Baquerolle Farm, but by mid-afternoon they have linked up with the 2/7th Warwicks on their left, and the Berkshires on the Brigade right. The latter have their headquarters on the Robecq crossroads. Last into position are the Gloucesters, who fortify St Venant and St Floris on their left flank.

*He visits each position throughout that long afternoon. One advantage of the dense smoke from the burning ammunition dump is that the Germans are denied observation from their balloons. Their artillery continues to pour fire into the area, but it is random. The roads and fields around Robecq are thronged with unmilked cows, geese, goats, hens and pigs, abandoned by their owners in their hurried flight. An exception is a little old French lady whom he discovers sheltering in a shell hole under cover of a large umbrella. He salutes, and presses on.*

*He is satisfied with the positions, and tells the battalion commanders so. They are pleased that they have reached the standard that this small but imposing man imposes. Small he may be, they reflect, but in him beats the heart of a lion.*

*He reaches his headquarters just as dusk is falling, to be met by Howitt. Unusually for this impassive man, his face looks troubled.*

*'Sorry to tell you, Brigadier, we have just had the most extraordinary order from Corps. We are to move back about a mile, and make a new line across the Robecq-St Venant road.'*

*'The devil we are. What do Division say about it?'*

*'I cannot find anyone above Staff captain to talk to. Apparently the GOC and the GSO1 are touring 182 Brigade's positions.'*

*'Have you sent a warning order?'*

*'Yes, Brigadier.'*

*'Send another message round that no move, I repeat no move, is to take place without my personal order, and that will not be before the whole Brigade have had their evening meal. No rear reconnaissance parties are to*

*move either. I will find General Colin and stop this nonsense.'*
*The order is cancelled, and he rises even higher in the estimation of his staff.*

On the morning of the 13th, there is a dense mist, under cover of which the Germans attack St Floris and Robecq. The Gloucesters at St Floris, and the Oxfords at Robecq, put up a stout defence. The fighting centres on Baquerolle and Boase's Farms, both of which are resolutely held, and the enemy falter and fall back. The defeat of this attack by rifle fire from small isolated posts has a most heartening effect on the new members of the Brigade. The Gloucesters are able to stand down half the battalion, who move into billets in St Venant. The cellars there are well stocked with good wine, which has lain untrammelled by war's alarms until now.

The fighting ebbs and flows throughout the 14th and 15th, until by 16 April it can be said that the tactical situation is stable. That night the Gloucesters relieve the Oxfords, who move back to the dubious comfort of St Venant. The next night the Germans make a determined attempt to take Baqerolle Farm, now held by the Gloucesters. A determined counter attack, led by a NCO, Sgt White, retakes the farm, capturing seventeen prisoners and a machine gun.

The Battle of Hazebrouck is over.

*France, 20 April 1918*

*Dear Brigadier*
*I hope this gets to you, although you are only a few miles away, things are in a bit of a muddle as regards mail and communication generally. First, may I say how thrilled we all were in the 28th when we heard of the doings of the 184th during the last few days. As CSM Biddle said 'Those Huns bit off more than they could chew when they took on our Patsy.'*
*You may have heard that, not long after I took over from you, we were pretty busy, at a place called Festubert. It lies just to the west of La*

Bassée, and you may remember it from '17. The Huns attacked on the 18th, and we had a warm time of it. Handford was on the left with A, then Mallett with B, and Seldon with D linked up with the SWB on our right. Smith had C in reserve. We knew what was coming from a German feldwebel we captured on the 17th, and sure enough at 4 am the next day the Hun bombardment opened. At 8.15 the infantry came over in the mist. All the telephone wires had been cut, but a runner from Mallett got through to say 'the Huns are making no headway and the Old Braggs have their tails up.' I thought you would like that.

Everyone was doing splendidly, but the one weak spot in our defence was a gap between the two halves of A Company's line. The Hun started to pour through here, and things were tricky for a bit, but young Hall threw out a flank and checked them. Fortunately for us the fog lifted, and now it was our turn to hand it out. Ammunition expenditure was prodigious, but we suffered from artillery firing over open sights. The Dressing Station was hit by a large shell, and the MO, Fairey, was all but buried. He only let us know about this when the show was over!

At the most critical time, we cobbled together a group of signallers, cooks, orderlies and batmen, and Smith took them out to the north end of the village, where they performed very well. You will be very sorry to hear that the Signals Sergeant, Cole, whom you recommended for a DCM, was killed in this party.

All our attempts to get through to Brigade were useless – we tried pigeons, but the first one went the wrong way, and the second was blown to bits by a shell – and at one stage we were literally fighting back to back. We were well supported by the Welch, who, with ourselves and some Camerons cleared Le Plantin. Once they realised that no further support was coming, the Hun began to withdraw, and we shot them down in droves. Some surrendered, including a German American who lit a cigar, put his hands in his pockets and announced that he was 'fed up.'

We took just under 200 casualties, and as you may imagine I am in the process of writing to scores of NOK. However, I felt I ought to write to you as soon as I could, to pass on the word that is going round the 28th: 'Patsy fought Festubert' they are saying, and of course they are right. I was privileged to command during the action, but the training, the philosophy, the spirit, all came from you. No wonder the Brigadier said 'All ranks fought as though mindful of the emblem they wear and fully

*justified the wearing of it.'*
*Please come and see us. Our best wishes from all ranks of the 28th, the*
*Old Braggs have their tails up! Your old comrade from South Africa days,*

*John Tweedie*

German shelling continues without respite. The tracks across the open fields which he uses to reach the front line positions are rendered especially unpleasant by the pernicious '106' fuzes with which the enemy is well supplied. From Robecq, through the Brigade position and back to St Venant, which is being steadily shelled to ruins, one takes one's life in one's hands to venture in to the open. His way usually leads him past the Asylum, said to be the second largest of its kind in France. From it, its protesting inmates are led to lorries and driven away.

On 23rd April he is at the Gloucesters headquarters at first light. They are to straighten out the line at Baqerolles Farm, at the same time as 183 Brigade attacks on their left. He is particularly keen to see that the artillery support they have been promised is on time and on target. Good communication is achieved for once by his Brigade Signal Officer, who lays a ladder line. The artillery support is so successful that the enemy are demoralised before the infantry get to grips. The operation is a complete success, bringing in seventy nine prisoners and a bar to Colonel Lawson's DSO.

Retaliation follows. The Germans have their old lines registered to an inch, and at noon they open a heavy bombardment, which continues until the 27th, when they launch their counter-attack. It is a half hearted effort. He joins the Gloucesters in the firing line, and takes joyful part in the turkey shoot which follows. A further sixty prisoners are taken.

The tide of battle is now flowing in the British Army's favour. He feels the euphoria of battle won. It is not a complete victory, and the cost has been heavy. In the last two weeks, the Brigade has lost sixteen officers and nearly 400 Other Ranks. But they have not yielded.

England is saved.

# Chapter 5

'On the whole, the objective set had not been attained. The attack had not penetrated to the decisive heights of Cassel and Mont des Cats, the possession of which would have compelled the evacuation of the Ypres Salient and the Yser position. No great strategic movement had become possible; the Channel ports had not been reached. Our troops on the left flank in the conquered trenches were in a very unfavourable situation, as they were strongly enfiladed by the British. The second great offensive had not brought about the hoped-for decision.'

General von Kuhl, Chief of Staff to German Army Group North.

## 184th BRIGADE DEFENCE SYSTEM

The Brigade is holding the right sub-sector of the Divisional front. The ROBECQ-CALONNE road and the rivers CLARENCE and NOC, lined with cottages and orchards run centrally down the Brigade front. Its flanks are open flat country.

The Brigade is concerned with two systems of defence

<u>The Forward System</u> This consists of

Front Line – about 1,000 yards in extent, well wired and consisting of a series of posts.

Support Line – about 300 yards in rear of front line, and on the right about 50 yards in rear of the COURANT DE MESSESEQUE. It is a more or less continuous shallow trench, but not yet wired.

Reserve Line – about 1,000 yards in rear of front line, well wired and a continuous trench, but in need of revetment and parados.

Strong points arranged in depth round selected farms and enclosures capable of breaking up attacks down the line of the road and rivers or of commanding the flat ground on either flank.

<u>The AMUSOIRES System</u> This consists of

An outpost system around the thickly wooded country and cottages as far east as CARVIN FARM – this takes the form of posts in covered and commanding positions.

Main line – about 1,000 yards in extent and stretching from the LA BASSÉE CANAL on the right to a point just south of the orchards of LES AMUSOIRES on the left. It is composed largely of a series of old earth breastworks – these are being joined up.

Support Line – about 500 yards in rear of main line. This consists only of a series of disconnected breastworks.

Reserve Line – running from LALMAU on the canal to LES AMUSOIRES and forming aswitch behind ROBECQ in case of enemy penetration to the south. Very little work has yet been done.

All troops of the Brigade are available, if required, to fight east of the AMUSOIRES line. Before entirely vacating that line, however, a nucleus garrison would be provided from Divisional troops. The essence of the defence of the Brigade sector is to maintain at all costs the strip of wooded country running down its centre. This strip is organised for flank defence so that it can be self-supporting as long as the AMUSOIRES system holds, and can deny the open ground on either flank to the enemy. In case of local penetration by the enemy, the front battalions will re-establish the forward system by immediate counter-attacks. All ranks must realise the value of instant action in this close country and the danger of delays. All plans for each locality will be cut and dried beforehand.

Withdrawal Arrangements

In case the enemy breaks through the forward system, the following exist in rear

AMUSOIRES System – this joins up with a similar system of the right Division.

BUSNES-STEENBECQUE system running east of BUSNES and manned by a nucleus garrison of Corps troops, who are also responsible for the canal bridges.

LILLERS-STEENBECQUE system running east of LILLERS and HAN, manned by a nucleus garrison of the troops constructing it.

The bridges over the LA BASSÉE Canal have been prepared for demolition. Units will send officer representatives to each bridge they are likely to use to indicate when all their troops have crossed it.

All forward troops of the Brigade are within the Alert Zone, and respirators will be worn accordingly.

5th May 1918                             BRIG GEN A W PAGAN, DSO
                                        Commanding 184th Infantry Brigade

The Brigade is now able to revert to the system of reliefs, but because there are only three battalions, each does four days in reserve, followed by eight in the line. Considerable shelling goes on from both sides, eventually becoming heavier from the British gun lines. The stream of shells passing overhead is everlasting by day and night; if it stops, men wonder what has gone wrong. The French inhabitants are still afraid to return, but their houses provide good comfortable shelter. At La Pierrière, whither the reserve battalion repairs for its four days of comparative ease, a well stocked canteen is set up, and beer, cigarettes and English papers are available.

The grass grows lushly in the Spring sunshine, and becomes so long that movement around the Brigade area is possible by day. Perhaps it is this that induces Lawson, commanding the 2/5th Gloucesters, to crawl forward once too often towards the German lines. His ensuing death is widely lamented.

There is pressure to obtain information on the enemy's identity, strength and intentions.

**184th INFANTRY BRIGADE ORDER NO 176     12th May 1918**

**The 2/4th Battalion Oxfordshire and Buckinghamshire Light Infantry will carry out an operation on the night of 13th/14th in order**
  **(1) To obtain identification**
  **(2) To inflict casualties on the enemy**
**The operation will be supported by Artillery and MG barrages.**

**The objective is the farm and enclosure known as ORCHARD FARM.**

**ZERO is 11.55 pm.**

**From Zero to Zero plus four minutes the Artillery barrage will be on the line q.14.d.1.5 to q.15.d.o.5. This lifts at Zero plus four, and from Zero plus four to Zero plus 20 minutes becomes a box barrage. 4.5 howitzers on roads and selected**

points in rear from Zero to Zero plus 20.

The Raiding Party will be formed up ready to start immediately outside our wire by Zero hour. At Zero plus 4 minutes Raiding Party will advance on its objective.

All ranks of Raiding Party are to be provided with 'Raid Identification Discs.' All badges and identifications are to be removed, and no documents carried. Prisoners and identifications are to be sent to Brigade with the least possible delay.

Watches will be synchronised at 8 pm tonight at Brigade Headquarters.

A J Howitt, Capt, Brigade Major

184th INFANTRY BRIGADE, BRIGADE COMMANDER'S INSTRUCTION

All intelligence from prisoners points to the certainty that the enemy intends to make frequent raids on those sectors of the Front which he is not actually attacking, with the object of keeping in touch with our order of battle, and preventing us from drawing off reserves to fight elsewhere.
These raids must be carefully watched for and all ranks must be impressed with the necessity for vigilance in meeting them. The following steps will be taken:

Patrolling will be active, and in addition to specific reconnaissance and fighting patrols, front line wire must be frequently checked.

The question of Listening Posts in Front must be carefully examined, especially in the neighbourhood of high standing crops in 'No Man's Land.' It may be necessary in some cases to cut these crops. If this is not done, Listening Posts lying in the near edge are the safest protection.

The look-out in Forward posts must be rigidly enforced, and any shortcoming found on the part of sentries in this matter severely dealt with. The importance of this is not at present realised by the young soldiers who form so large a proportion of the present garrisons. Each man must keep his rifle close to him,

# Chapter 5

ready for use at all times. In this matter also the young soldiers need constantly reminding of the power of their rifles.

5th June 1918                                                  A W Pagan, Brigadier General

As June lengthens, the pressure on the British front eases, as the Germans transfer their attention to the French sector. Another menace now threatens both sides. Initially labelled PUO – pyrexia of unknown origin – Spanish Flu will eventually kill more Europeans than the war. It hits 184 Brigade as they are preparing further operations to test German intentions. It starts with the Oxfords, and by the end of June has resulted in 250 men from the brigade being hospitalised. Their comparative fitness, and superior rations, saves them from the worst effects of this mass killer.

Offensive operations must be maintained, and higher formations demand more and more frequent indications of German morale and fighting capability. One method to assess this is the Trench Raid.

**Account of RAID by 2/4th ROYAL BERKSHIRE REGIMENT on night 23/24th June 1918**

**Strength of party: 1 Officer and 35 other ranks**
**Objective: Orchard at G.8.w.d.5**

Party was formed up outside our wire. A gap was cut in the German wire about 20 minutes before the barrage commenced. The party got to within 20 yards of the German wire before barrage lifted, and when it lifted entered the orchard by the N.W. Corner, leaving one man at enemy's wire to guide the party when returning.

A N.C.O and 4 men went about 40 yards to the left to protect the flank, and the remainder turned right inside the orchard, and proceeded along the parados of a trench running along the front hedge of the orchard and close to it. This trench was covered with hurdles in places. Party went about 30 yards along this trench and found a considerable number of Germans in the trench. One put up his hands, but the others did not, and the Raiding Party opened fire at point blank range. A number of Germans were hit, but they did not open fire for a short time. When they did, the officer of the Raiding Party was hit at once and fell and did not move again.

A considerable number of Germans now began to come down both sides of the orchard, and the Party withdrew by the gap, covered by the fire of their Lewis gun. At the same time, a number of Germans began to come up from the left. One of them was shot, and the remainder stopped. There were a considerable number of tools lying about near the trench, so possibly the presence of a working party may account for the presence of so many Germans in the orchard.

The wounded men, three, were got away but the officer could not be got away. He was probably killed. A good number of Germans was killed or wounded but no identification was obtained.

> A W Pagan
> Brigadier General
> Commanding 184th Infantry Brigade

*'There will be hell to pay with Division, if they find out that you were with the Raiding Party, Brigadier.'*

*'Better make sure they don't know, then, Howitt! We move out of the line tomorrow, and life is going to be pretty quiet for a while. Better get some good training organised.'*

*'Yes, Brigadier.'*

*'Funny, you calling me Brigadier. I was talking to the French Liaison Officer at Corps the other day. I said 'Je suis Brigadier,' and he laughed – why do you think that was?*

*'No idea, Sir,' replies Howitt, too tactful to point out that Brigadier in French means Corporal of Horse.*

# Chapter 6

For the next six weeks, the Brigade enjoys a quiet life behind the lines. Platoon and company training, bayonet fighting, patrolling and the attack are practised, and give notice of the way in which the war is slowly turning. The Brigade is moved to the Second Army, and plays its part in the massive deception plan that will herald the British offensive at Amiens.

There is time also for less military activity, and a Brigade Athletics Championship is held, involving boxing, cross-country, relay race and tug of war. The Brigade Commander supervises.

Reconnaissance parties familiarise themselves with areas where the British offensive, when it comes, may be expected to concentrate.

As a final preparation for the open warfare that is anticipated, each battalion holds a field day, with a narrative supplied by Brigade Headquarters.

### NARRATIVE

The Germans having been heavily defeated on a wide front are retiring in a N.E. direction, and are being vigorously followed up. Their retirement is on parallel roads. They are holding high ground above LINGHEM to cover retreat on Road to LAMBRES and AIRE. It is reported by our cyclists that this force is out of touch with the forces on its flanks. 184 Brigade is ordered to deal with this force.

Aeroplanes report 12.30 pm enemy commencing to dig in on line BLUE. From movement seen in front there is reason to believe that some posts are being dug in advance of this line.

**OXFORDS have secured a footing on W. edge of high ground and are reorganising.**
**GLOUCESTERS and R. BERKS are ordered to carry out the attack.**

*'Brigadier, there is a Captain Lavender to see you.'*

*'Is there, by Jove! Show him in. It's good to see you, Lavender. How are you, young man? Fully recovered from your wound I hope?'*

*'Fully recovered, thank you Sir, and keen to get back to proper soldiering.'*

*'Proper soldiering, eh? What is wrong with the Donkey Wallopers?'*

*'Nothing, Sir, they are a splendid lot, and they have been very kind to me. But I am really in a training role, and we all know that the cavalry are not going to get a proper look in, not here in France.'*

*'So, how can I help?'*

*'Well, Sir, I thought you might find some use for me with the 2/5th.'*

*There is silence as he considers.*

*'They have a vacancy for a captain in C Company. How do you fancy that? I think we can fix it. Just don't tell too many people how it was done!'*

On 7 August, 184 Brigade resumes its place in the line, as intelligence comes in that the Germans are retiring from their outpost line, possibly even north of the Lys Canal. The Brigade is ordered to support an operation by 182 Brigade to occupy Courtrefoie Farm, overlooking the canal. The two forward battalions, Oxfords and Gloucesters, are to move forward to align the Brigade front with whatever success is achieved. Two platoons of Oxfords, without artillery support, take the German lines along with four prisoners and a machine gun. At the same time the Gloucesters send out strong patrols to the Plate Becque, without contacting the enemy. This feature, a muddy stream varying in width from twenty to twenty-five feet, and of uncertain depth, is to be the scene of the Brigade's next operation on 11 August.

# Chapter 6

## 184th INFANTRY BRIGADE ORDER NO 204 by BRIGADIER-GENERAL A W PAGAN

The 184th Infantry Brigade will cross the PLATE BECQUE and establish a Bridge-head on 11th August.

The attack will be carried out by the 2/4 ROYAL BERKSHIRE REGIMENT on the right and the 2/5 GLOUCESTERSHIRE REGIMENT on the left.

ZERO hour will be 4.15 am.

The attack will be supported by Artillery, Machine Gun barrage, and by Trench Mortars.

The ground won will be consolidated in depth. Particular attention will be paid to the left flank.

24 ft bridges for crossing the PLATE BECQUE will be carried up during the night of 10/11th August to the starting positions, in the following proportions:

> Right Battalion – 2/4 Royal Berkshire Regiment – 8
>
> Left Battalion – 2/5 Gloucestershire Regiment – 8

Contact aeroplane marked with a small black square projecting from the rear edge of each of the lower planes, will call for <u>RED FLARES</u> at the following times: 8 am, 11 am, 4 pm, 7.30 pm.

Advance Brigade H.Q. will be at STATION INN

> R S Lindsay
> Captain
> A/Brigade Major

## OPERATIONS CARRIED OUT BY 184th INFANTRY BRIGADE

### August 11th 1918

The 184th Infantry Brigade attacked under an artillery barrage with a view to establishing a bridge-head over the PLATE BECQUE.

One and a half companies 2/4th Royal Berkshire Regiment attacked on the right and two companies 2/5 Gloucestershire Regiment attacked on the left. The majority of the attacking troops got across the PLATE BECQUE up to their barrage with the exception of two platoons whose bridges broke or did not fit.

The enemy were holding the place in great strength with numerous machine guns, and, despite the barrage, opened fire at once. The attacking troops had no room for manoeuvre and at once suffered heavy casualties. The attack failed and the attacking troops withdrew.

The ground was held in great strength and the barrage was apparently not heavy enough to keep down hostile fire. Provided the enemy is in strength, an attack on the PLATE BECQUE would have to be made on a much wider front, with much greater artillery preparation.

**A W Pagan**
**Brigadier-General**
**Commanding 184th Infantry Brigade**

In late August the Brigade relieves 183 Brigade as the Advanced Guard Brigade of the 61st Division. German prisoners confirm that the enemy has been ordered to fall back gradually to a Main Line of Resistance, running from the Lys Canal to Estaires. The division is to take part in King Albert's Flanders Offensive.

The German guns are still active in the dismal dyke-ridden country. Round Estaires and La Gorgue they are busy blowing up and burning anything that could possibly assist an advancing foe. Black palls of smoke rise from mills and factories; church towers and spires vanish; and booby traps are prepared at road and rail crossings, and in the few buildings that are at all habitable.

On 27 August, the Oxfords and Berkshires are ordered to attack in support of the 40th Division on the Brigade's left flank. The attack is initially successful, and the line is advanced, with little interference from German artillery, but well-sited machine guns take a heavy toll. At dusk the Germans counter-attack, and the Oxfords are forced to abandon their hastily prepared defences.

Despite these signs of German stubbornness, an air of cautious optimism pervades the Brigade. A sense of being on the threshold of great things is abroad.

# Chapter 6

<u>184th INFANTRY BRIGADE. PROVISIONAL INSTRUCTIONS IN THE
EVENT OF ENEMY WITHDRAWAL</u>     28th August 1918

In the event of a further German withdrawal the advance will be continued
by definite bounds.
<u>First Bound</u> – to line COBALT COTTAGE – WANDLE FARM
Outpost Line of Resistance will be moved forward to Line BISHOPS
CORNER – RUE MONTIGNY – CHAPELLE DUVELLE
Battalions will take forward with them their M.G. Sections, Trench Mortar
Sections and Royal Engineers sections.
Battalions will consult with Battery Commanders as to the employment of
Artillery.
Brigade H.Q. will move to Factory K.23.0

> R S Lindsay
> Captain
> A/Brigade Major

# WAR DIARY OF 184th INFANTRY BRIGADE 1918

28th August. Patrols of 2/4 Bn Royal Berkshire Regt pushed forward after
daybreak and occupied CRINQUETTE LOTTE without opposition from the
enemy. Patrols also pushed forward in the direction of OBOS COTTAGE
but this was found to be occupied by the enemy. Enemy artillery was quiet
throughout the day and the shelling was mostly by 77 mms on the forward
area.

29th August. At 1.30 pm the Division on the left attacked and at the same
time the 184th Inf Bde pushed forward patrols under cover of a light
barrage. Good progress was made with only slight opposition from the
enemy. Two prisoners from 187 I.R. and a light machine gun were captured
by a patrol of the 2/4 Royal Berkshire Regt.

30th August. Patrols again pushed forward along the whole Brigade
frontage without much opposition from the enemy. Bde HQ moved to
MERVILLE.

31st August. Progress was made during the day and close touch was kept
with the enemy. Opposition from the enemy was considerable on the front

of 2/4 Royal Berkshire Regt.

Further orders with regard to enemy withdrawal and objectives of the Brigade issued. Patrols are to be pushed forward on the whole front and are to keep in touch with enemy continuously and, wherever they are able, are to push straight on to the objective. Battalion Commanders are to use the Artillery and trench mortars at their disposal to this end.

1st September. Patrols pushed forward along the whole of the Brigade frontage. Up to 4.30 pm there was some opposition and the 2/5 Gloucester Regt had some sharp encounters with the enemy. The 2/4 Royal Berkshire Regt passed through Estaires with only slight opposition from the enemy in the eastern part of the town. The 2/4 Bn Oxford and Bucks Lt Inf moved forward with close support in the evening.

2nd September. There was considerable opposition from the enemy, and our patrols which tried to cross the River LYS were prevented from doing so by parties of the enemy with M.G.s holding the eastern bank of the canal. During the afternoon there was considerable hostile artillery activity.

3rd September. Brigade relieved as Advanced Guard Brigade by 182nd Brigade, and moved to area of ESTAIRES.

4th September. Battalions ordered to move forward at 4.30 pm in order to conform with the withdrawal of the enemy.

## REPORT ON THE ATTACK CARRIED OUT ON THE MORNING OF THE 12th SEPTEMBER 1918 BY 2/4th OX & BUCKS LT INFTY

OBJECTIVE. To capture JUNCTION POST and trenches in the vicinity, and establish posts.

STRENGTH OF ATTACKING PARTY.

      2 Platoons of A Company, 2 Platoons of C Company.

      2 Platoons of D Company as supports if needed.

ZERO. 5.15 am.

NARRATIVE. The Assembly was successfully carried out under difficult weather conditionsand the Attacking Party moved off under cover of an Artillery Creeping Barrage. Our M.G.s and Lewis Guns opened up a heavy fire on their flanks with a view to keeping the enemy M.G.s out of action.

The enemy was on the alert and immediately brought a heavy M.G. fire to bear on our line. Owing to bad light and rain the enemy apparently did not see our attacking troops until they were quite close upon them, but the cross fire from their M.G.s caused considerable annoyance to our troops.

At 5.27 am a rocket was fired from BARTLETTE FARM which evidently called for the barrage of 77 mm and 4.2 H.E. which came down on the orchard and the road beside it. This slackened down at 5.40 am.

At 5.50 am very heavy M.G. fire was opened on our troops from BARTLETTE FARM.

At 6.1 am bombing was heard on the right flank of the attack and it was reported that a section under Corpl. WILCOX, A Company, had surprised a battery of 4 enemy M.G.s (3 heavy and 1 light pattern). These were bombed and fired upon with rifles, killing the personnel working the guns (2 men per gun). Before moving on up the trench, the guns were put out of action by putting a round through the breech casings.

The Section then moved up the trench, driving the enemy before them. In face of an enemy counter-attack of 25 to 30 men, the Section had to withdraw.

Citation for the Victoria Cross for Corpl WILCOX follows under separate cover.

> A.W. PAGAN
> Brigadier-General
> Commanding 184th Infantry Brigade.

On 15 September, the Brigade is relieved, and spends some days in reserve among the fields and orchards west of Sailly-sur-la-Lys. Life is full of incident, from the daily attentions of German light guns, to the explosions of buildings prepared by the retreating Germans. In Estaires a house goes up nearly every day. A cross-roads in the centre blows up just after the Assistant Provost Marshal passes, to mutterings about 'poor timing' from those who have suffered the attentions of the Military Police. The Oxfords' water cart is blown up while refilling, but only the horses are hurt. A farm near Montigny blows up seventeen days after the Germans have withdrawn.

On 27 September, the Brigade issues further instructions for action in the event of an enemy withdrawal. Stressing that battalion headquarters should ensure that their affiliated gunners are co-located with them, it also details an elaborate system for collating all information, both enemy and friendly forces, and disseminating it as rapidly as possible to all concerned in what is expected to be a fluid and fast moving situation. Lucas lamps, the latest in a series of expedients for passing information, are recommended, but the use of any and all means of communication possible is emphasised. It concludes, 'The advance must be vigorously pressed, and must never be held up because a flank unit is held up.' However, on the same day, orders are received that Junction Post, the scene of Corporal Wilcox's heroism, must be taken.

*'Junction Post is the key.' The Divisional Commander's words ring in his ears as he leaves the General's Headquarters for the two miles to his own Brigade Headquarters. He knows enough of the objective to appreciate that it has many advantages for the defender. A grass bound breastwork, it commands good fields of fire, but lies just beyond a slight ridge which denies our gunners direct observation.*

*After much thought, he decides that the operation will be best carried out by a single battalion, at present in reserve; the Gloucesters are the obvious choice; their CO, Christie Miller lacks experience, having been in command only a few weeks, but he can be relied on to carry out his orders, and he has some excellent company commanders, who can act on their own initiative as the situation unfolds; detailed orders will therefore get the Battalion on to the objective, but after that success will depend on the leadership of sub-unit commanders; some support will be required from the battalion at present holding the line, and the Berkshires will provide that. But he needs time to prepare and rehearse. He must somehow inculcate in the 2/5th all the knowledge and experience that he has gained in three and a half years of front line warfare.*

*He issues his orders on the 27th. The attack will be carried out in three days time, by three companies in line, arranged in depth. The fourth company will follow closely until they reach the old*

German line, which they will clear, and then establish supporting posts for the new line. The Berkshires will push forward parties on both flanks of the attack, and establish posts to conform with the Gloucesters' final positions. Battle wire-cutters and bombs will be issued generously.

Two days of strenuous preparation follow. He selects an area near Estaires which resembles the lush grassy terrain surrounding Junction Post, and for two days the Gloucesters rehearse the attack until they can do it unprompted. On the night of the 29th, they move forward. It is very dark, and they have difficulty in finding the Berkshires' posts, but by first light they are in position, and the supporting barrage falls, rather erratically at first. From his position to the rear of an orchard which contains Miller's headquarters he watches in dismay as shells fall on the left and centre of the forming up place. He turns angrily to the gunner lieutenant colonel beside him, who in turn speaks urgently in to his telephone.

Once the Gloucesters cross the start line, there is little to tell him of progress except the roar of artillery and the angry clatter of machine guns. The intention is that C Company will attack Junction Post, A will take the ground to the left, and D the right, establishing four platoon posts in the trench system connecting to the objective. B Company is to be in reserve.

A trickle of walking wounded, and a handful of German prisoners give a meagre account of the fighting. It appears that Junction Post has been taken, but a bombing attack by the Germans on the left has forced a withdrawal there, and the situation is not at all clear. All day the noise of battle continues, with no clear indication of success or failure. At nightfall he moves forward to the Gloucesters headquarters.

He finds little enlightenment from the Gloucesters' Adjutant, but as he waits, Christie Miller stamps into the shelter. He sets out the situation. 'Junction Post is in our hands, but it will not be held for much longer if we do not regain the enclosed ground to its west. Harvey is dead, we've taken quite a few casualties but tails are up. A good push in the morning should do the trick.'

'If I may suggest, Old Man...C Company are well lodged; use C Company Commander to take two platoons from your reserve and take that enclosed ground. No need for artillery support – they cannot observe in to that area and our guns would be as big a risk to you as to *the Germans.'*

*Miller nods, and turns to his Adjutant. 'Make out a message, Tom, and let me see it before it goes.'*

*At 0630 the next morning, the counter-attack goes in, and by early afternoon the area around Junction Post is secured. As he moves forward to congratulate the exhausted troops, he passes a party of walking wounded escorting a dozen prisoners. One of the wounded has his arm strapped to his chest, and is walking with difficulty.*

*'Good show, Lavender, I knew you would crack it. Worth a bar to your MC I would say.'*

*In his report, he writes, 'The Glosters fought with stubborn determination, and their success under great difficulties, and where others had failed, was a very fine effort.'*

### 184th INFANTRY BRIGADE ORDER NO. 251 by Brigadier-General A.W. PAGAN, DSO

The 184th Infantry Brigade will attack the enemy's positions, tomorrow 2nd October, at BARTLETTE FARM, and will consolidate and hold the line. Flanks will be joined to our own line.

2/4th ROYAL BERKSHIRE REGIMENT will carry out the attack.

Zero will be 05.45 2nd October, 1918.

The attack will be carried out under a Field Gun and Howitzer barrage, and will be supported by Heavy Artillery, Trench Mortars and Machine Guns. After the objective has been gained patrols will push forward.

Contact aeroplanes will fly over and call for Red Flares by Klaxon Horn and a white flare at 0700, 1030 and 1900.
Leading Troops only will light Red Flares. Aeroplane markings – a black square on the rear edge of the lower planes.

42nd Squadron R.A.F. are arranging for a counter-attack machine to be in the area at about1201 to attack any ground targets observed in the neighbourhood of above operations.

In the event of an attack, Special SOS signals, as under, will be used.

Between 0600 and 1800 – Daylight Smoke SOS RED and BLUE

Between 1800 and 0600 – SOS Rifle Grenade RED over GREEN over YELLOW

Watches will be synchronised at 184th Infantry Brigade Headquarters at 2200 hours tonight.

> R I Lindsay
> Captain
> A/Brigade Major

## 184th INFANTRY BRIGADE WAR DIARY (1918)

**1st October.** The French method of writing times was taken into use, and all timings changed by one hour.

**2nd October.** At 0445 an attack was carried out against the enemy position at BARTLETTE FARM by the 2/4th Bn The Royal Berkshire Regiment. The attack was carried out under a field gun and howitzer barrage. There was no reply to this from the enemy's artillery and the objectives were easily taken. 4 prisoners of the 49 I.R. were captured. They stated that the enemy was in the process of withdrawing and that there were only weak rearguards left behind. Patrols were immediately sent out all along the Brigade Frontage, and touch was again established with the enemy, but little resistance was offered, and the Brigade reached the line FLEURBLAIR – CROIX BLANCHE by 1000 hrs. Orders were issued to move on immediately to the next objective. Progress was not so fast owing to the rough nature of the ground and the wide ditches. Opposition was only encountered from isolated machine guns, and this was soon overcome. There was no artillery fire from the enemy's guns except occasional shots from H.V. Guns.

**3rd October.** The advance was again resumed at 0700 to the next objective, which was the old British Front Line. Practically no resistance was encountered, but the going was difficult owing to the barbed wire and trenches of the old trench system. The next objective was the line WEZ MAQUART – MONT PINDO and the advance towards this objective was resumed at 1200 hrs. Opposition became more persistent after crossing the Old German Front Line, and was temporarily held up by machine guns.

Herewith extracts from the 61st Division Order No 216 dated 10th October 1918.

From all information at hand the enemy is carrying out a retirement on a large scale. A vigorous pursuit has been ordered along the whole Army Front. It is to be carried out with the utmost determination. The hostile rear-guards are to be attacked as soon as located. The one aim and object of all ranks will be to get at the enemy's main forces and to bring them to battle.

The 61st Division will be prepared to move forward at short notice. In the meantime, every advantage will be taken by all units in the Division of the excellent facilities and ground in their neighbourhood for training purposes.

**WAR DIARY OF 184th INFANTRY BRIGADE (1918)**

14th October. Brigadier-Gen A.W. Pagan DSO, who had been ordered to proceed to England for a tour of duty at home returned from the course at FONTAINBLEU together with Brigadier-General F.A.N. Thorne DSO (Grenadier Guards), who assumed command of the 184th Infantry Brigade. 15th October. Brigadier-General A.W. Pagan DSO proceeded to England.

# Chapter 6

*France*
*October*

*Dear Mother*

*I have surprising news for you – I am on my way home. No, I have not been unstuck! It seems that some clever fellow in the War Office has decided that anyone who has served longer than a certain time at the Front has to go home, otherwise they are liable to go doolally! So I hope to see you later this month.*

*You will be amused to hear that a few days before I left I attended the course at the Inter Allied Tank School – not much use to me now, but it could be in the future I suppose. Of course I am disappointed to be leaving, especially now that we have the Hun on the run. The end of the war cannot be far away, and the sooner it comes the better. The men have been magnificent, and it has been an absolute privilege to command such a splendid body. I will never let anyone do down the Territorials.*

*I cannot blame anyone for being cautious at this stage, nobody wants to be the last British soldier of the war to die, but our wonderful young officers continue to lead by example. They are so plucky. It is that spirit that has carried us through.*

*I had hoped to see the old 28th before I left, but no such luck. If I am honest, commanding a brigade has not been half the thing that command of the 28th was. I suppose I was fortunate to have three years of it. Perhaps I will command again, in peace time.*

*I will not be home straight away – I have to see some people in London. All very mysterious!*

*I will tell you all when I see you. My love to you and the girls*

*Yr very affec son*
*Alexander*

*London is grey; greyer than a Flanders dawn. Few young men inhabit the streets, which are the haunt of bustling women, old men and urchins. In Russell Square a news vendor displays his headline: 'The Vigilante demands Minister's resignation.' At the Senate Building, an over age private mumbles over the order requiring his presence. A boy scout guides him through the dimly lit corridors of the Ministry, to arrive at an office whose spartan furnishings mirror the fine features of its owner.*

*'Brigadier-General Pagan to see you, Colonel,' the boy announces breathlessly.*

*'General, what a pleasure. It is so good of you to spare me the time, I am sure you are anxious to get home. I believe we may have met before; I visited your regiment at Bloemfontein in '02 when I was working on resettlement for Lord Milner. The back-to-back boys. I much enjoy the poems of Ivor Gurney, but I think he would have moved on from the 2/5th before you commanded their brigade.' The faint Borders accent augments the impression of a genial host, but the tweed suit and air of authority make it clear who is the senior here.*

*'First, I should apologise for the air of muddle that you may detect around us. We are at a funny stage, the Minister is about to hand over, and the whole Ministry will be wound up within weeks. So I have asked you here to help me with a little task that I hope will soon be complete. You may know that I have been writing a history of the war, from the first months. It has been produced in instalments, and now that we are on the brink of victory I wanted to talk through the final stages with someone of your unique insight. I understand that you have been at the Front since January 1915, commanding a regular battalion and then a brigade.' A file is consulted 'Wounded three times, DSO, Order of Leopold, Croix de Guerre, mentions..., it's a fine record, probably unique. I wonder if we could have a little chat about one or two things.'*

*The conversation, stilted at first, slowly begins to flow more easily. The reorganisation of the brigades... the shortage of infantry... the lengthening of the Front... . At this stage the name of General Maurice is mentioned. The name means nothing to him, and the discussion moves smoothly on. The German Offensive of March... the extraordinary effect of the massed German artillery... the desperate cobbling together of individuals to repair shattered battalions... the hurried re-training of rear area men... Backs to the Wall... the first signs of indiscipline among the Germans, usually so professional.*

# Chapter 6

As he relates the deeds of his men, his usual reticence deserts him. The Lys, Hazebrouck, Festubert, the final efforts of an exhausted adversary, the realisation that the worst is over, the cautious feeling forward as the Germans prepare their withdrawal, the piercing of their line at critical points, the advance against little opposition. He stops abruptly, aware that his eloquence might seem like boasting. There is a reflective pause.

'Wonderful, I feel almost as if I am there. A final question for you, if I may, of a more general nature. The French Army mutinied, the Russians revolted, the Germans look as if theirs is falling apart, but our Army has survived with its discipline intact; what made our army so resilient? What was the glue that kept units together in the face of such terrible trials?'

'Regimental spirit. We have fine generals, fine young officers, splendid men, but it is the spirit of the Regiment that binds them together. Let us never lose it.'

'You have given me a lot to think about, and I am more grateful than I can say. Now, I have another gentleman for you to see. One of the curious aspects of my job is that I work with some people that the public seldom hear about. I am afraid you will not be told his name, but he will give you some rare and valuable insights that will help you in your next appointment. He will explain more. I expect you will have some leisure time during your leave for a little light reading, so I hope you will accept a copy of one of my novels. Curiously it is about a senior Army officer, and the extraordinary adventures he gets up to. I hope you will enjoy it.'

He is led down a labyrinth of corridors to a small office, where a large, cadaverous man with the pasty complexion of the indoors greets him.

'I am going to talk about the situation in Ireland, and particularly in Dublin. Please do not interrupt, I will be happy to answer any questions at the end. First, the political situation, and I am mainly concerned here with the extreme Nationalists, that is Sinn Fein, and its nucleus, the secret Irish Republican Brotherhood. The failure of the Easter Rising of 1916 convinced them that an open fight with the forces of the Crown was useless. They are therefore embarking on a campaign *of passive resistance in local government; meanwhile they are preparing for guerilla warfare. The body that is to do this is known as the Irish Volunteers, but they are increasingly being called the Irish Republican Army, and I will tell you more about them in a moment.*

*On the open political front, they have had only limited success so far. The war has been good for the farmers; the war has not disturbed them, there has been no conscription, and by and large people have been content to let matters be, particularly while so many men are fighting in France. This will change with the imminent ceasing of hostilities, and we can expect an increase in agitation, particularly in conjunction with the Irish Transport and General Workers' Union, which is heavily infiltrated by Sinn Fein. They have virtually swept the moderate Nationalist Party out of power.*

*You are no doubt aware that, since 1916, the military try civil cases by court martial, under the Defence of the Realm regulations. One of the articles of this act deals with illegal drilling, which has become widespread in the last year. Although Dublin has been largely spared, in every village in the south west parties are meeting for drill almost daily. They make every effort, including if necessary murder, to obtain the rifles of soldiers home on leave, and have built up large stocks. But the situation would have been containable, but for the declared intention of the British government to introduce conscription. You will appreciate better than most, General, how much the Army needed men in the last year, but although the move has been dropped, the possibility was seized upon by Sinn Fein, backed by the Roman Catholic church, as a rallying point. In August Sinn Fein issued an anti-conscription manifesto, and this has been read out all over Ireland, often by senior figures in the church. Over the last few months the membership of Sinn Fein has increased by fifty five to sixty per cent, and the IRA has become more active, intimidating the civilian population, and carrying out small scale attacks on the police.*

*The Irish Republican Army is established on similar lines to any other army. There are brigades, battalions, companies and half-companies, each with a Commander, an Adjutant, a Quartermaster, an Intelligence Officer and so on, the difference with a regular army being that posts are filled by election. They rely for funds largely on the United States, where those of Irish descent are generous in providing the wherewithal for their campaign of intimidation and propaganda. By setting up their own parallel system of civil administration they aim to show the world that we do not have the situation under control.*

*Now for our position, and first the police. There are two police forces, the Dublin Metropolitan Police and the Royal Irish Constabulary, and they are fundamentally different. The DMP, as its name implies, covers the metropolis only. Its officers are unarmed, and the force is modelled largely on Robert Peel's lines. The important point for you is that their outlook is quite different to that of the RIC. They do not regard themselves as servants of the British state, and many of them are actively sympathetic towards Sinn Fein. They have a small political G Division, who take their life in their hands every time they go to work.*

*The Royal Irish Constabulary are a very different kettle of fish. They have a quasi-military ethos, with barracks, carbines, and an army style uniform. But it is worth acknowledging that until recently arms were carried very infrequently, and the barracks were often just small country police stations with a day-room and a few bedrooms. In general they are still well regarded in the community. Their duties are summarised as 'Crime Ordinary' and 'Crime Special', the latter dealing with political affairs. Each County Inspector sends a lengthy report on these matters each month, and it is these reports that provide most of the intelligence on which the Governor acts.*

*As for the military, they are at present divided in to four districts, of which yours, Dublin District, covers both Dublin city, policed by the DMP, and the RIC's own Dublin and Wicklow Districts. Your legal staff, responsible for courts martial under the Defence of the Realm Act, for want of anyone else, are becoming more and more involved in intelligence matters. No doubt you will be looking at your organisation, and assessing whether it requires some amendment in light of what is certain to be an increasingly turbulent time.*

*There, I think that is quite enough for now. You will of course receive further briefings when you arrive in Dublin – I believe you take over on the sixth of November. If you have any immediate questions, I will try my best to answer.'*

# Chapter 7

*The few days in England have flown by; a hurried visit to Cheltenham, an hour with his tailor and lunch at his London club, but otherwise his time has been spent on a frantic round of interviews, briefings and conferences. A very great man has been most complimentary about his time in France, Military Operations, Military Secretary, Adjutant General, Military Intelligence, all have wanted their pound of flesh. A mass of information whirls through his mind, but the message from the Great Man is clear, 'It is going to be a war, but not a war like you have been fighting in France. It will be a war against an unseen foe, and you will have one arm tied behind your back. Remember, this war will be won or lost by politicians, not the Army. Your job is to hold the ring while they sort it out. God help you!'*

*The train chugs slowly through the West Country to Holyhead and the ferry. Nicholls has gone ahead, and is at the quayside to meet him, with his staff car and driver. He half listens as Nicholls expands on his domestic arrangements. It seems that the Residence will be a distinct improvement on the shattered farms that have been his lot for four years. He notices the extreme youth of the sentries on the dock gates, and comments on them.*

*'Wait till you see the rest of the troops. There are Young Soldiers Battalions, then there are cyclist battalions, yeomanry, odds and sods, and most of them can't wait for demob. They hear the news from France, and all they can think of is getting home before the milkman gets off with their missus. 'Course there's the Berkshires, regular battalion, they are alright.'*

*Over the next few days he is immersed in a whirl of visits and briefings. Opinions on Sinn Fein, the IRB and the IRA are many, varied, and often contradictory. They are moderate and reasonable people; they are politically driven with a hatred of the English that rules out any compromise. They lack organisation; they have a very well developed intelligence arm, every movement of Crown Forces is noted, every man in the RIC is a potential target. They are the unemployed, the ne'er do wells, who would never have joined any political movement if it had not been for the move to apply conscription to Ireland; they list poets, writers, artists, and intellectuals among their number.*

*The two and a half thousand men under his command, which embraces Counties Dublin and Wicklow, are a far cry from the efficient, disciplined but war-weary soldiers of the 28th and 184 Brigade. The Young Soldiers battalions are composed of fine material, they turn out well on parade, handle their arms smartly, and are keen to do well, but they are completely unversed in the arts of modern war. The Yeomanry and Territorial units will, he has been assured, be gradually replaced by regulars, but the Adjutant General has warned him that Ireland is low on the list of priorities for demobilisation. Already, as 1918 draws to a close, there are murmurings of discontent in France at the slow rate of release of men who have endured months of savage fighting. He decides to hold a District shooting competition. It will be the Victory Rifle Meeting, and it will give him the opportunity to address the hierarchy of all his units, in a suitably martial setting, at which he can lay down his priorities. With typical generosity he pays for a suitable trophy for the Champion at Arms.*

On 21 January 1919 the 'Dail Eireann' assembles at the Mansion House. The twenty-nine Sinn Fein MPs present a pledge to work for the establishment of an independent Irish Republic, accepting nothing less than complete separation from England, and abstaining from attending the English Parliament. A declaration of Irish Independence is read.

**INSPECTOR GENERAL'S REPORT FOR JANUARY 1919**

I have to report that in the month of January there was no improvement in the state of political unrest which pervades the whole country.
Considerable progress has recently been made by the Irish Transport and General Workers Union. Its officials and members are mainly Sinn Feiners, representing the Socialist and Labour wing of the Irish revolutionary movement.

# Chapter 7

__TIPPERARY.__ On Jan 21st, at midday, at Soloheadbeg, close to Tipperary, 2 constables were shot while escorting 160 lbs of gelignite to the County Council Quarry. Both constables were fully armed, but the attack was so sudden that they were killed before they had a chance to defend themselves. The assailants took the police rifles and ammunition. A council employee who was present cannot or will not identify the assailants.

__DUBLIN__ On Sunday 19th January at about 2 pm a party of 50 Sinn Feiners drilling in the Dublin Mountains near Dundrum attacked a police patrol of 2 men, whom they disarmed and tied up.

At Belmont Camp 12 bayonets were stolen on 24th January, but as 19 soldiers occupied the hut where they were kept, collusion is suspected.

The sum of all this intelligence does not amount to definite information that an outbreak will actually take place, but it shows a dangerous state of unrest, and preparation for revolutionary action which necessitates every possible precaution. While an adequate military force is maintained in Ireland it is improbable that armed rebellion will be attempted. Having repeatedly threatened to make government impossible, and having now established the 'Dail Eireann' the republicans may be expected to make some demonstration of their boasted power. Meanwhile in cases of illegal drilling, unlawful assembly and incitement to sedition, the law is enforced by prosecuting the offenders who invariably claim to be citizens of the Irish Republic and deny the authority of the court.

*As winter turns to spring, he takes whatever opportunity he can to explore the countryside outside Dublin, and into County Wicklow. He can combine duty with pleasure, an official visit to the Worcesters at Portobello with a reconnaissance of the Avonmore or the Dodder, the East Surreys at Collinstown with a visit to the loughs at Bane and Lene. During a visit to DMP Headquarters he mentions his interest in fishing.*

*'Tommy's the man for you, he knows every salmon and trout river in this part of Ireland. Let me introduce you.' He is taken to a large office in Great Brunswick Street, where officers in plain clothes sit at desks, telephoning, typing or discussing in low tones. All conversation ceases as they enter.*

# Gloucestershire Hero

*He senses an atmosphere of caution. This is the haunt of secrets, here men's lives are scrutinised, not for what they do, so much as what they think. 'Welcome to G Division.' He is introduced to a dozen men, some openly friendly, some indifferent, some he feels resent his presence; he is the representative of Crown Forces.*

*He gets in to the habit of an afternoon stroll through the centre of Dublin. He is usually in mufti, but always an armed and watchful Nicholls is a few steps behind him. He occasionally drifts in to the Capel Street Library, where he looks for the books of his interlocutor from the Information Ministry in London. He chances on two men, who give the impression that they would have avoided him if they could.*

*'It's Broy and Neligan, isn't it?'*

*They gape at him.*

*'Never forget a face or a name; if you were in my Regiment I would know your numbers!'*

*They avert their gaze.*

*'Come on Ned, we're best away. Excuse us General.'*

*He mentions this chance encounter to Tommy when they are next on the river. It is still early for trout to show much activity, and the salmon run is late this year. They spend as much time on the bank chatting as they do on the water.*

*'You have to realise that we are all under a wee bit of pressure in G Division. Most of us have recently had a warning from the IRA – resign or take the consequences. Funnily enough, Ned Broy and Davie Neligan were the only two who did not get the word. I'll be honest with you, General, I sometimes wonder where the biggest threat comes from, outside the office or in it.'*

*'What is your answer to the threat, Tommy?'*

*'I took me oath to the Old Queen, and to her heirs and successors, me eldest was killed at the Somme with the Munsters – oh yes, he heard all about Patsy Pagan of the Gloucesters – and me mo'er always said to me, "Tommy, when you have given your word, don't ever break it." So, there's your answer, General.'*

# Chapter 7

On 7th April, Broy smuggles the IRA leader, Michael Collins, into the G Division archives, where he shows him the photos and personal details of Broy's colleagues. He is signing their death warrants.

**INSPECTOR GENERAL'S REPORT FOR MAY 1919**

Sinn Fein continue to espouse the doctrine of allegiance to an independent Irish Republic, headed by 'Dail Eireann'. This doctrine has been circulated by handbills, and is expounded at length in the manuscript of a speech taken from Mr J A Burke MP by District InspectorHunt (since murdered) at a meeting on 25th May, for which Burke will be tried by court martial when the police can effect his arrest.

There were very few raids for arms, but it is reported that efforts are being made to purchase arms and ammunition from soldiers.

In consequence of information received that an extensive raid had been planned in the vicinity of Dundalk by Sinn Feiners for the night of 4th June, military assistance was requisitioned by the police, certain roads were picketted by soldiers, and a commercial traveller motoring to Dundalk who failed to stop when challenged by a sentry was unfortunately shot with fatal effect.

Seven lbs of gelignite, together with a revolver and gun, a bullet mould and a quantity of ammunition was seized by the police in Wicklow. The person in charge, an Irish Volunteer, has been tried and convicted by court martial.

A most important step for the British army is taken when, for the first time, they begin to develop intelligence of their own. The impulse comes from the determination of a group of agents to place their services at the disposal of the Intelligence Officer at GHQ, rather than the police, whom they no longer trust. From this group a considerable amount of information about Sinn Fein and the Irish Volunteers is obtained. A military post is established to collate the information from this group, the officer who sets it up is joined by others, and they soon expand the meagre knowledge of both police and military. They are placed under the control of Dublin District.

In June, the first attack on a DMP constable is made, and towards the end of July, the first member of G Division is shot and mortally wounded. His death is the first of six directly attributable to Broy's treachery.

**INSPECTOR GENERAL'S REPORT FOR AUGUST 1919**

Printed notices were found posted up in several counties, declaring that the police are spies and traitors and should be treated as traitors, and warning people in the name of the Irish Republic not to speak to them or in any way tolerate their existence.

Needless to say in the face of such terrorism witnesses cannot be induced to come forward and give evidence against the criminals. In some counties it has been necessary to concentrate the police; some outlying barracks have been vacated and the remainder fortified for defence.

Some private houses were raided for arms – 3 persons were made amenable – and 19 rifles consigned to the military were stolen from the goods store at Greenore Railway Station during the night of 2nd August. None of them has been traced, though the surrounding country has been thoroughly searched.

<u>County Dublin, County Inspector's Report for August 1919</u>

Portions of the County are not in so satisfactory condition as in other months. As to the Sinn Fein activity there have been six cases of Raiding for Arms carried out by a gang of young men who go about at night armed with revolvers and wearing masks. The task of the police in dealing with this gang is very difficult, as the members come from the City and there are many roads and byways by which they sneak up and assemble in some pre-arranged and evidently lonely spot. Short particulars of the indictable offences follow.

1. <u>Robbery of Arms.</u> On 6th August a party of 6 men wearing masks entered a house at Kilmamanagh and took away a shot gun. The raiders were armed with revolvers, but none were identified. RIC and DMP searched the house of a suspect named O'Gorman and found 4 military service revolvers and Sinn Fein literature. The DMP reported case to the Court Martial Authority.

2. <u>Demand for a Robbery of Arms.</u> On 7th August a masked and armed party called at the house of Mary Dempsey, Bluehill, and demanded 'Hands up or we fire.' They had revolvers in their hands. The party consisted of about 7 young men, none of whom can be identified.

3. <u>Robbery of Arms.</u> On 14th August a group of 6 or 7 raiders called at a house in Gallowstown. They gained admission by knocking in the ordinary way, then put on masks and swarmed all over the house. The occupant had previously had a small arsenal of arms, but had handed them to police. No identification has been possible.

4. <u>Robbery of Arms.</u> On 20th August during the absence of Private Stedman with his regiment his residence was entered by 2 armed and masked men who carried off a German Mauser revolver Stedman had brought from the Front.

5. <u>Raid for Arms.</u> On 24th August the house of a DMP pensioner was raided. He handed over a service revolver. The raiders were masked and armed with revolvers.

6. <u>Raid for Arms.</u> On 24th August a party of 7 or 8 armed and masked young men who stated they were 'soldiers of the Irish Republic' knocked at the door of a house in Gallowstown. They searched the house and took away a shot gun and 24 cartridges.

Since the beginning of last week plans have been made for joint military and police patrols of some strength which move about quickly and scour the roads frequented by this gang. These patrols have met with some success already.

*Late August in Dublin. Once the streets of Gallowstown are dark they fall silent. The only ones out will be up to mischief. He steps quietly in to the small barrack, Nicholls beside him. He recognises the Head Constable by his warrant officer badge. They nod to each other; this is his third visit in a week, and no words are necessary.*

*An hour passes, two, the monotony broken by an occasional tumbler of something dark and fiery. He is about to depart when the door bursts open, and a dozen men push inside. Military khaki and RIC uniform green contrast with the informal garb of the young man they have secure in the grip of two constables.*

*'We got him, Sir, no doubt what he is up to. He had a loaded revolver and mask on him, and a Sinn Fein pamphlet.'*

*The Head Constable looks closely at the young man, no longer struggling. 'I know this one.'*

On 7 September the first serious attack involving loss of life is made on the Army. A party of fifteen soldiers of the King's Shropshire Light Infantry is about to attend the Wesleyan Chapel at Fermoy. They carry rifles but no ammunition. As they enter the chapel they are fired on by a group of forty rebels, who make their escape in motor cars. Private Jones is killed, and others wounded.

The inquest returns an open verdict.

**INSPECTOR GENERAL'S REPORT FOR SEPTEMBER 1919.**

**According to information from various sources Irish Volunteer Head Quarters has directed all County Commanders to hold a certain number of men armed and in readiness to execute orders to attack barracks and assassinate police.**

**No doubt very many Irish Volunteers now belong to the IRB, an oath-bound society started in 1869 to establish an Irish Republic. Murder and outrage dogged the footsteps of this Secret Society until it was banned by the Roman Catholic Church. Its aims are identical to Sinn Fein, but unlike the latter its existence is invisible.**

# Chapter 7

It is obvious that the existing political unrest throughout the country is of a very serious nature; in a large area the police without the assistance of troops would be totally unable to maintain any semblance of order, and any reduction of the military garrison would be fraught with grave consequences.

*Autumn at Dublin Castle, where the weekly Commander's Conference is in session.*

'Operational matters, Brigade Major?'

'Sir, joint patrolling with the DMP and RIC continues, the three battalions on Op Immediate provide ten sections each. Briefing and marry up with the police takes place at the designated barracks... Briefing of patrols... Police or Army lead... Procedure on arrest... Guards and escorts... Instructions for raids... Vehicle protection... Check points... Protection against surprise... Walking out... Out of Bounds Areas...

'Thank you, Brigade Major. Now for Administrative matters...'

*The conference proceeds along well rehearsed lines. The relief of a Young Soldiers' battalion, the movement in and out of drafts to keep overseas garrisons up to strength, health, support for the few wives that accompany their men folk, the forthcoming District Athletic Championships, the start of the Rugby Football season. At the mention of Rugby, he sits up a little straighter in his chair.*

*After an hour and a half of routine matters, he sums up, and then turns to a new subject.*

'Gentlemen, we have said little so far about Intelligence. From what I have learned over the last nine months, Intelligence is the key to the situation. We are not at war, so I am not talking about Intelligence as we used to know it in France – or Mesopotamia,' he adds hurriedly as he sees the look on the Staff Captain's face. 'Our operations must be based on good intelligence, otherwise we just swing around blindly, and upset a lot of perfectly peaceful folk in the process. We have relied on the DMP for guidance as to Where and When, but if I am frank, the other unknown, the Who has been missing. I am happy to say that this fault is to be addressed, both within the DMP and within our own organisation. So I want to introduce to you two gentlemen who are going to assist us. The first is Mr William Redmond, who is the new head

*of G Division of the DMP. The second we will refer to as Major Sykes;*
*that is not his real name, and in theory he does not exist, but he will be in*
*charge of Intelligence on our staff, maintaining close liaison with*
*Mr Redmond, and working directly to me. Chief Clerk, please show the*
*two gentlemen in.'*

The appointment of Redmond marks a major turning point in the campaign. His predecessor, through his long service in Ireland, had a good general knowledge of the various secret political organisations in the country, and his registry was sufficiently well organised to enable him to compile a reasonably satisfactory report on such matters. Neither his training, his system or his mentality induced him to go further than this, or to take active steps to watch the growth of Sinn Fein or the activities of the Irish Republican Brotherhood. When several of the best detectives of G Division were murdered the work of this branch was restricted more and more. After a report by Sir B. Thomson, the Superintendent in charge is placed on retired pay, and Redmond, an RIC officer from Belfast, comes in to reorganise G Division. One of his first steps is to request that the Army set up a parallel organisation, with whom he will work closely. Unfortunately, although he soon realises that there is a serious leakage of intelligence from within his organisation, he is unable to stem the leak before his own murder some months later.

*Delhi Barracks*
*Catterick*
*30 October 1919*

*My Dear Patsy*
*I was quite astonished to receive your letter. I knew of course that you*
*were due to return to the 28th at some time, and I rather assumed that*
*you would take over from me in command. That is what I would wish,*
*what the whole regiment would wish, and I know it would be your*
*dearest wish. These damned cuts! I know major generals who are now*

*lucky to command battalions, and I heard the other day of one of our most distinguished brigade commanders who has gone back to his regiment as a rifle company commander.*

*So what to do? I hear from AG that you leave Ireland some time in November, and it is then up to me when you should report. The fact is, as you of course know, that we move to Tidworth next month, so there is no point in you coming here. If you cannot command the 28th or 61st, the Depot seems the obvious post. Ingram hands over in February of next year, and the whisper is that you will take over. So, how would you fancy a long leave until then? You deserve it if any man does. It would seem the most sensible course all round. Much as I would love to have you with us, it is hard to place a Brevet Lieutenant Colonel in the Battalion.*

*We are in good heart, as ever, although the constant dribble of men leaving us to keep the 61st up to strength is unsettling. But the Rugby is well under way, and we have a very promising side, if I can only hang on to the key players!*

*Do let me know if you are happy with this plan. I hope to see you at the Regimental Dinner, and if there is any way in which I can help, please let me know.*

*Yours Aye*
*Francis Nisbet*

## STATEMENT BY THE INSPECTOR GENERAL 14 NOVEMBER 1919

The country is in a very rotten state. Nationalists and probably the majority of Sinn Feiners would be glad of a peaceful settlement, but the Irish Volunteers and other extremists persist in their demand for complete independence. They are saturated with hostility to British rule, and should they receive a general order to give trouble it would no doubt be obeyed, the police would be overwhelmingly outnumbered and the situation would necessitate strong military action.

Within a year after the Armistice, the great military machine the British have created is almost entirely dismantled. Conscription is ended. The professional horizon of regular officers shrinks from the complex management of technological war to the life of the regiment, to small wars in Iraq, Palestine, Persia, Russia, and to duties in support of the civil power in India and Ireland.

In 1919, at the suggestion of the War Secretary, Winston Churchill, the 'Ten year rule' is adopted: the services have to base all their future planning on the assumption that there will be no major war for ten years. The army is thus in the position of a colonial *gendarmerie* with no major role to play or plan for.

Owing to the small size of the army that remains after swingeing cuts, there is a bottleneck in promotion. Senior officers earn advancement even more slowly than before the Great War. The nation itself loses all interest in defence. A strong tide of pacifism flows against war, and even against soldiers themselves. The very existence of even a comatose army seems indecent to public opinion. To say that the commanders, such as Haig, were stupid and callous offers a convenient explanation of the length of the war and its human cost. No one can accept that these were the inevitable results of the collision of two roughly equal coalitions of industrial nations intent on outright victory. To a public accustomed to the tiny casualties involved in previous wars, the British figure of three quarters of a million dead, though half the French figure, and one third of the German, seems unthinkable. Not only the number of casualties, but the segment of society on which they fell, is unthinkable. The British middle classes had been spared the levée en masse of France, or the universal conscription of Germany and Russia, and so the Great War dead of all classes must be attributable to the incompetence of the generals; and from distrust of the generals, to the public's distrust of all soldiers is a short step.

Recruiting and retention, always buoyed by recruits from rural Ireland, become very difficult. A trickle of recruits continues to come from the traditional sources, but as the twenties draw on, recourse is increasingly made to the lowering of standards. The Regimental Depot of the Gloucestershire Regiment is located at Horfield Barracks, Bristol. It is almost adjacent to the magistrates court, where a recruiting sergeant is always present to affirm that His Majesty would accept a certain young man, if his offence is not too grave, and if Their Worships would be pleased to consider seven years military service a suitable alternative to a more traditional penalty.

*'Escort and Accused, quick march, leftrightleftrightleftrightleft wheelmarktimehalt! Right turn! Recruit Wilkins, Sir.'*

*'Wilkins, you are charged with absence without leave, under Section 13 of the Army Act 1881, in that you at Horfield Barracks, Bristol, were absent from 1800 hours on Tuesday 12 May to Monday 18 May 1921. Time absent six days.'*

*'Well, Wilkins, are you guilty or not guilty of the charge?'*

*'Guilty, Sir.'*

*'The offence is reported by 19417262 Corporal Evans. Evidence please, Corporal Evans.'*

*'Sir, at 0800 hours on 12 May, I called the roll of Salamanca Platoon. I noted that Recruit Wilkins was absent, and placed him on report, Sir. I called the roll each day until 18 May, at which time Wilkins was present for the first time.'*

*'Do you dispute the evidence, Wilkins?'*

*'No, Sir.'*

*'Before I pass sentence, I should like to know a little about the circumstances. You are from the Forest of Dean, I believe, Wilkins?'*

*'Yes, Sir, from Clearwell.'*

*'So why were you absent for six days?'*

*'Sir, 'tis sheep shearing time at home, and my Nan said I should help out, else she wouldn't be able to feel right with the village. We'm always done our bit at sheep shearing, and times is hard, like, she needed the money I could get. I knew I was supposed to be on parade, like, but I couldn't argue with our Nan.'*

*'Captain James, what is your report?'*

*'Colonel. Wilkins has done well on the course. Like all Foresters, he is very stoical, but has his own ideas on some things. He is due to pass out in two weeks, and is listed for the draft for the 2nd Battalion. This is his first offence of absence, and I would recommend leniency, Colonel.'*

*'Well, Wilkins, Captain James has spoken up for you. But you must realise that absence is a serious offence. In some circumstances it might be*

*considered desertion, and desertion in the face of the enemy carries the death sentence. Your offence is not of that order, but you must learn a lesson from this. I am going to make sure that you are on that draft for the 28th, so you are sentenced to fourteen days confinement to barracks.'*

In 1923 an important change is made in the establishment and syllabus of training of recruits. The new system is named the Maxse Scheme, after the general commanding the corps under whom 184 Brigade served in 1918. The whole system of recruiting is changed, and instead of being carried out by counties or regiments it is to be done on an area basis. All infantry recruits are to be despatched as they enlist to the particular depot of the area open to receive them. When a squad of thirty is formed, another depot forms up the next squad. Men who have some definite claim on a particular regiment are still, in theory, permitted to enlist in the regiment of their choice, but the general result is that the percentage of county men in a regiment reduces. Although for the Gloucestershire Regiment the figure remains high, the scheme causes considerable misgivings.

Until the Maxse scheme was introduced, my regiment had no difficulty in getting recruits; when I finished command of the Depot in 1923, our height standard was 5'7". I am convinced recruiting would be vastly improved if the Maxse scheme were abolished. Each county would then have to produce its own recruits. The territorial spirit is engrained in most counties; if a man has some hope of going to his own regiment we should get more of the better class of recruit.

I am also opposed to the granting of discharge at the seven year point. I meet many of them around the county who have had to go at the end of seven years when they want to extend.

A.W. Pagan
Lt Col, OC Depot

# Chapter 7

Sir

I am directed to inform you that approval is given to the posting of Major (Brevet Lieutenant Colonel) A.W. Pagan, DSO to 1st Battalion the Gloucestershire Regiment as a supernumerary officer, and to state that this officer has been ordered to be prepared to move to Cologne to report for duty not later than 10th August 1923.

Kindly report the date he assumes duty.

I am
Sir
Your obedient Servant
D. Forster, Colonel, for General
Adjutant General
11th June 1923

'RSM Griffin, Sir, welcome home, it is wonderful to see you back. The Warrant Officers and Sergeants' Mess would be honoured if you would dine with us next week.'

'Of course, I should be honoured. How are you, and how is Mrs Griffin? And two daughters if I recall correctly. Tell me, how is Cologne as a station? How do they enjoy it?'

'I think a lot of us are going to miss it when we move to Aldershot in two months. We have done a lot of good training in the hills and woods a few miles out of town, and we have made a good name for ourselves for work and sport – especially Rugby football! You are going to be shocked, though, when you see the size of the companies. Germany does not qualify as overseas, so the Second Battalion is getting all the drafts, and we are about four hundred below establishment.

My family has certainly enjoyed Cologne. We must have visited a dozen castles, and we have lived very well, with special allowances and privileges. We also have the Cologne Post, which is good for the men and the wives.

*It is hard to see the civilian population suffering, but they did bring it on themselves. Personally I think the Kaiser should have been hung, instead he's living like a lord in Holland, while your ordinary Fritz is near starving.*

*Now, how are you Sir? Last time I saw you was at Messines, just before I got my Blighty one. We all presumed you would be coming as CO, but I suppose these things take their time to come through. Meanwhile we shall have two colonels.' He shakes his head. 'Funny situation.'*

*'I am a company commander, no more, no less. It will be good for discipline, RSM, good for discipline!'*

In October 1923 the 28th move to Aldershot, where they join 5 Brigade. Recruiting continues to be hard, and it is difficult to take soldiering seriously in an atmosphere of continuing financial stringency. Regimental tradition provides the backbone to stiffen the sinews of all ranks from bemedalled commanding officer to newest joined private soldier.

*Waterloo Barracks, Aldershot, May 1924. Headquarters Company of the 28th is holding Company Commander's Orders.*

*'Whom do we have today, Company Sergeant Major?'*

*'Just Private Wilkins, Sir, charged with absence.'*

*'Ah, yes of course, sheep shearing time in the Forest.'*

*'I beg pardon, Sir, how do you know that?'*

*'Never mind, Sergeant Major, never mind. Bring him in.'*

### THE BACK BADGE, JOURNAL OF THE GLOUCESTERSHIRE REGIMENT, 1925

Colonel Pagan has, during his 26 years with the Regiment, devoted not only his time, but every ounce of energy he possesses, to the well-being of the Regiment. He will be remembered by thousands as the

# Chapter 7

Officer Commanding the 28th during one of the most critical periods of its history, and his cheerful spirit, combined with the splendid example he set all ranks, will remain in the history of the Regiment for all days.

Regrettably, his days as a regimental officer are drawing to a close, but we congratulate him on his promotion, and wish him well in his new post as Assistant Commandant at the School of Musketry. As the Army grapples with new ways of doing things, it is comforting to know that hard won experience and plain common sense will be applied to the education of our young officers and non-commissioned officers.

The Small Arms School, or The School of Musketry, as it is still called by traditionalists, established at Hythe, Kent, in 1919, is the centre of the Army's expertise in infantry weapons. Here, young officers and NCOs are given a thorough grounding in the theory of small arms fire, the practical application of theory into practice on the ranges, and the instructional techniques for ensuring that all infantrymen are skilled in the use of rifle, bayonet, revolver, Lewis Gun and Mills bomb. The aim is to train the trainers, so that their men can attain the rate of fifteen aimed rounds per minute with the bolt action Short Magazine Lee Enfield No 1. The course is intense, and the senior NCOs from the Corps of Instructors of Musketry are merciless in correcting their young charges. The standard to which they aspire is that of the old Regular Army of 1914, whose small arms fire at Mons halted the German Army.

One of the main duties of the Assistant Commandant is to move the Machine Gun School from Netheravon, on the disbandment of the Machine Gun Corps. The Vickers machine gun will now revert to its pre-war role as a critical support weapon in the infantry battalion.

# Gloucestershire Hero

Headquarters
Small Arms School
23rd June 1928

Dear General

1.  As Colonel Pagan's appointment as Assistant Commandant at Hythe expires on 1-2-29, the question of his future career must soon come under consideration. I am therefore writing to bring to your notice the good work which he has done as Assistant Commandant at Hythe, and his fine qualities as a soldier.

2. The tenure of his appointment at Hythe has coincided with an important change in the organisation of the Small Arms School, which has added materially to the responsibilities of the Assistant Commandant. During this period there have been important developments in our system of Small Arms Training to meet the requirements of modern developments. Colonel Pagan's energy, capacity, loyalty and intimate knowledge of the requirements of the army have been invaluable throughout.

3.  He is a man of sound judgement, marked personality and with undoubtedly great power of command. He combines an extraordinary knowledge of, and sympathy with, Regimental requirements, with sound military knowledge and balanced views. He is essentially a soldier. He would in my opinion make a first rate Brigade Commander. He would be ideal as the Commander of a Territorial Brigade of his own Regiment, as his life is wrapped up in his Regiment, and its associations, and his influence in this direction is probably almost unique. His personality and military qualities mark him down as an officer who will be considered for promotion when his time comes.

4.  I attach a digest of his services in peace and war which shows that Colonel Pagan is a soldier who has been well tried out. He is now only 50 years of age and full of energy and keenness on his profession.

# Chapter 7

Yours Sincerely
E. McKenna

Major General H.H.S. Knox, CB, DSO
Director of Military Training
The War Office, London, SW1

31 October 1928

Sir

I am directed to inform you that approval is given to the appointment of Colonel A.W. Pagan, DSO as Commander, Rangoon Brigade Area, Burma Independent District, in succession to Brigadier R.E. Solly-Flood, CMG, DSO, and to state that this officer has been ordered to be prepared to embark on or about the 5th January 1929, to take up duties accordingly.

Kindly report the day he assumes duty.

I am, Sir, Your obedient Servant

D. Forster, Brigadier, DMS for

Major General, Military Secretary

His Excellency,
The Commander-in-Chief in India,
Military Secretary's Department,
Army Headquarters,
India

27 November 1928

Sir

With reference to War Office letter of 31 October, I am directed to inform you thatthe appointment of Colonel A.W. Pagan DSO as Commander Rangoon Brigade Area, Burma District, in succession to Brigadier R.E. Solly-Flood CMG DSO has been cancelled. Approval has been given for Colonel Pagan to command the 10th (Jubbulpore) Infantry Brigade in succession to Major General C.J.B. Hay CMG CBE DSO, Indian Army, and that he has been ordered to be prepared to embark to take up duties accordingly on or about 7th January 1929.

Colonel Pagan is granted the temporary rank of Brigadier from 18th February 1929. Army Headquarters India have been informed accordingly.

I am, Sir, Your obedient Servant
Forster, Brigadier DMS for
Major-General Military Secretary

The Under Secretary of State
(Military Department)
India Office
London SW1

**MEMORANDUM**     From Lloyds Bank Ltd, 6, Pall Mall, SW1
To The Secretary, War Office, SW
28th Jan 1929

<u>Col. A.W. Pagan</u>

The above named officer relinqd. his Staff appt. as A/Comdt S.A.S. 8/1/29 vide Ldn Gaz. D/15/1/29 upon embarking for India 7/1/29. He was granted leave from 21/11/28 to Embarkation for India. Including the 24 days leave, this officer received during July and August his total leave to embarkation amounts to 71 days. In

view of the attached certificate please confirm our issue of full Staff
Pay to 7/1/29.

> (Sgd) F.C. Codrington
> Manager

From F.2. War Office
To Lloyds bank Ltd (Cox & King's Branch)
As this officer completed 61 days leave on 27/12/28 he was only
entitled to Staff Pay equal to half pay (Art.421) after that date, up
to 7th Jan.
You should therefore effect recovery of the amount over issued

> (Sgd) H.A. Hayward

*He has been in India for two months, and he is not happy. He is fifty one
years of age, and has never been away from the green fields and hedgerows
of Europe before. It is all utterly alien. The heat, the dust, the squalor, the
beggars, the temples, the caste system, the ceaseless movement of men and
animals combine to make him feel that he is a visitor from another world.*

*His soldiers are impressive, the men of his three Indian battalions
tower over him, they are grim and professional, volunteers all, true and
loyal servants of the Raj. But he cannot speak to them. Sikh, Dogra or
Jat, he has not a word of their language. Sepoy and Sowar, Naik and
Lance-Naik, Havildar and Rissaldar, Subadar and Jemadar, Jemadar
Major or Wordie-Major, their thoughts are closed to him. His munshi
is in despair.*

*'Brigadier, Sahib, your efforts are like the poet Callwell said; his
Hindustani words were few – they could not very well be fewer, just idharao,
and jaldi jao and khabadar you soor.'*

*He envies the officers, many the third or fourth generation of their family
to serve in India. They converse fluently in their soldiers' tongues, and
with civilians in the lingua franca of Hindustani. Even with them he is on
unfamiliar ground. Pay and conditions, leave and privileges, discipline and
terms of service, all are unfamiliar. Their war was not his war. His service
was in France, theirs in Palestine and Mesopotamia. He remembers Aubers
Ridge, the Somme, the Lys, Passchendaele, they talk of Jerusalem and Gaza,
of Kut and Baghdad.*

*With his English battalion, relations are easier. But the Fusiliers have been in India for six years. For them life revolves around cold season training, hot weather hill stations, home leave, and The Club. Perhaps if he were married, The Club would be easier. He remembers the old adage, 'Subalterns may not marry, Captains may marry, Majors should marry, Colonels must marry.' A wife would smooth his appearances at the centre of European social life, would play tennis, bridge and croquet, would enjoy the tea dances, would, above all, give him entree to the world of gossip and intrigue which surrounds their little world. He painfully negotiates the world of tiffin, of stengahs and club sodas, of calling cards, strict social etiquette and horses, polo and gymkhana. He knows nothing of pig sticking, of shikar and mahseer, of mahout and maneater. In fact he sometimes thinks the young generation laugh at him, find him an object of amusement, because he is not familiar with the land, with the language, with the rituals. They contrast him unfavourably with his predecessor, a 'Piffer' of many years service in India. He is often asked what he intends to do in the hot weather. 'Are you married, or do you live in Ooty?' they ask archly and grin. 'Will you be going to a hill station?'*

*He does not answer. He is not going to a hill station. He is going home.*

From: Brigadier A.W. Pagan, DSO
Commander Xth (Jubbulpore) Infantry Brigade
Jubbulpore

To: The General Officer Commanding
Deccan District
Bolarum

Sir,
I have the honour to request that I may be permitted to retire, on retired pay, at as early a date as possible.
I completed 30 years service on February 11th, 1929, and 8 years in the rank of Colonel on January 1st, 1929.
My reason for this application is that my private affairs necessitate my presence in England as early as possible and for an indefinite period. My address in England will be:
Army & Navy Club

# Chapter 7

Pall Mall
London S.W.

I have the honour to be, Sir,
Your obedient servant
A.W. Pagan
25th April 1919

**REPORT OF ARRIVAL IN THE UNITED KINGDOM**

| | |
|---|---|
| Rank and Name: | Brigadier A.W. Pagan |
| Date of Embarkation (India) | 18-5-29 |
| Port of Embarkation (India) | Bombay |
| Port of Disembarkation (United Kingdom) | Plymouth |
| Date of arrival (United Kingdom) | 6-6-29 |
| Cause of return to United Kingdom | Leave pending retirement owing to private affairs. |

# Chapter 8

*On the east side of Gloucester lies Upton St Leonards. In 1930 it is a pleasant village of some one hundred souls. On top of Upton Hill on the western side is Upton Knoll, a pleasant, stone-built Victorian house set in five acres overlooking the Severn Valley. Beyond can be seen the Welsh mountains, the Forest of Dean, and further north the Malverns and Worcester. The garden is well stocked, and contains a wealth of unusual trees and shrubs planted by the Bellows family. Their successor, Canon Brewster, is happy to sell to the senior military man who turns up on his door step one day, and particularly admires the stone lion which graces his front lawn. He mutters something about it being close to a sphinx, and therefore a sign that the house must be meant for him.*

*Just down the hill is the gardener's cottage, and he is delighted that the gardener will stay on to work for him. But he needs a house for Nicholls, who announces his intention of marrying Liliane, his childhood sweetheart from Dursley. The solution is to build Yew Tree Cottage, in the grounds of Upton Knoll. From there Liliane can reach her precious salmon fishing, and Harry can attend to him and his car. For the car, and a love of fast motoring, become his passion.*

*In 1931 he is appointed Colonel of the Gloucestershire Regiment in succession to General Sir Frederick Shaw. The appointment is a largely ceremonial one, but he has the responsibility of guiding the affairs of the Regiment as a whole. He is a sounding board for many, and particularly the Commanding Officers of the two regular and three territorial battalions. He can listen, he can offer a sympathetic ear to those with troubles, either personal or military, he can advise, he can direct the work of Regimental Headquarters, he chairs the annual Regimental Dinner, he is in touch with the royal Colonel-in-Chief, he chairs the Regimental Association, the Council and the Trustees.*

*The Back Badge notes that he is somebody who has the energy, real keenness, and the backing of everybody to look after the regiment's interests. 'Colonel*

199

Pagan is not only good in peace, but he is good in war, and no more gallant officer has ever entered the Gloucestershire Regiment.' Admired, honoured, respected and held in huge affection by all members of the Regiment, he does not, unfortunately, hold the same position in the councils of the Great and the Good. He is not of the Brotherhood of Camberley; he has not attended the Staff College, the two year course for ambitious officers which is so important for their future employment. He could have taken the entry exam before the war, his three years with the Militia would have been the ideal time. But time spent on the Staff would be time away from regimental duty, and that is the end of the matter. So, when it is a matter of defending the Regiment's interests, whether it is in lobbying for an officer to be given advancement, or in matters of uniform or precedence, or, above all, for the posting and employment of the battalions, his voice lacks weight. He is not known by the members of the Army Board; he has not spent one or two years alongside the commanders and staff officers he has to impress, above all in the departments of the Adjutant General, and the Military Secretary. Serious repercussions are to follow.

These are difficult times for the two regular battalions. The thirties are a time of economic hardship for Britain, and the Army is still subject to the Ten Year Rule, and its accompanying economies. Pay and conditions are appalling, recruiting accordingly falls away. The Second Battalion, the old 61st, based at Catterick, has to be reduced in numbers to keep up the strength of the First Battalion, the 28th, in India. When the 61st are moved at short notice to Mersah Matruh to replace a garrison unit reinforcing Palestine, they can only muster 280 all ranks, against a war time establishment of 800. They have just enough men to administer themselves, and the Commanding Officer writes in despair, 'We are just wasting time; in the circumstances I am desperately anxious to bring them home.'

The trials and tribulations of the Regiment apart, life is pleasant. He can entertain at Upton Knoll, where Harry Nicholls and Liliane help him keep an immaculate household. He is made a Deputy Lieutenant of the county, and in this capacity welcomes the new Colonel-in-Chief, the Duke of Gloucester, when he assumes the appointment in 1935. He is honoured at his old school, where he becomes a member of College Council, and one of his delights is to watch the Cheltenham eleven on sunny afternoons on the Close. But his greatest diversion is to drive, at great speed, a series of extremely powerful, and extremely fast, motor cars.

# Chapter 8

**METROPOLITAN POLICE
CONFIDENTIAL REPORT**
D Division
Paddington Station
29th August 1936

Report for the information of the Under-Secretary of State, War Office, Whitehall respecting Brigadier-General Alexander William Pagan.

On 26th August 1936, Brigadier-General Alexander William PAGAN, of 'Upton Knoll', Upton St Leonards, Gloucestershire, appeared at Marylebone Police Court, before Mr Boyd, Magistrate, and was fined thirty shillings and his driving licence was endorsed, for exceeding the speed limit of 30 m.p.h. in a built up area, con. to Road Traffic Act 1934, Sec.1. It is not known whether Brigadier-General Pagan is still on the Active List.

In the late thirties, strange things are happening to the Territorial Army, and the 4th (City of Bristol) and the 6th Battalions of the Gloucesters are run down further and further, until their annual camps become little more than Old Comrade reunions. In 1938, the 4th Battalion is converted to 66th Searchlight Regiment, Royal Artillery, and the 6th Battalion to 44th Battalion Royal Tank Corps. The Colonel of the Regiment has no say in the matter, and is not even consulted when there is a move – ultimately nugatory – for the two units to retain the Back Badge.

'But it is impossible that the Back Badge, the most distinctive badge of the Gloucestershire Regiment, be worn with the badge of another unit. Had I, as the Colonel of the Regiment, been consulted in the matter, as I should have been, I should have been able to prevent the unnecessary expenditure.'

A.W. Pagan, Brigadier,
Colonel, the Gloucestershire Regiment

*His spirits are lifted by the result of the Army Rugby Cup, won for the second time in the Regiment's history, by the 61st, now stationed at Plymouth. Cheering them on from the touch line, he notes two young officers, Heidenstam and Arengo-Jones, who play a prominent part in this victory. A few days later, Arengo-Jones requests an interview; still a second-lieutenant, he wishes to marry.*

'How many motor cars do you have?'

'Two, Sir.'

'Well, my advice to you, young man, is to get rid of one of the cars, and the girl at the same time.'

To: Lieutenant Colonel The Hon N. Somerset, DSO, MC
Commanding, 2nd Battalion The Gloucestershire Regiment
Plymouth August 1938

Dear Nigel,
Congratulations on your appointment. If there is one thing that gives me comfort at this dire moment in our Nation's fortunes, it is the knowledge that the 61st is in good hands. One word of advice. The War Office has some odd ideas sometimes. Whatever happens, do not be inveigled into trying to lessen Regimental Spirit. You have a good battalion, more imbued than most with Regimental Spirit. If you destroy that spirit you will wreck the battalion.
Yours Aye
Patsy

# Chapter 8

## HEADQUARTERS SOUTHERN COMMAND, SALISBURY

To: The Under-Secretary of State, The War Office, London S.W.1
31st July 1939

Sir,

I have the honour to refer to War Office letter P/724/13 M.S.2 (T.A.) dated 17th July 1939, in which the re-appointment of Colonel and Hon. Brigadier General A.W. Pagan DSO to the Territorial Army Reserve of Officers (National Defence Companies) was disallowed, because he is over the retiring age.

I applied for the re-appointment of Col. Pagan DSO because I consider his services as the Sub-Group Commander of National Defence Companies to be raised in the Counties of Gloucester and Worcester would be invaluable at the present juncture.

Not only is Colonel Pagan unusually young and energetic for his age but he is a bachelor and has considerable leisure which he devotes whole-heartedly to the interests of all organisations, both service and ex-service in this part of the Southern Command. He has been Colonel of the Gloucestershire Regiment for 18 years and is undoubtedly the personality which commands the greatest respect and co-operation of all, civil and military alike, for military purposes in Gloucestershire. He has already, in anticipation of his N.D.C. appointment being approved, done a great deal of work in connection with it.

At this critical time, when the recruitment of officers and men for the National Defence Companies and their organisation is one of the greatest problems in this Command, I consider it would be a calamity to reject Colonel Pagan's invaluable assistance and experience. In this connection I would draw attention to Notes on the Conference on N.D.C. Matters held at this Headquarters at the special request of the Director of Military Operations at the War Office, which were forwarded under this Headquarters letter S.C.5/18346 (A) dated 20th July 19139, particularly para.5.

I accordingly request that authority be given at a very early date for the re-appointment of Colonel and Hon. Brigadier-General

A.W. Pagan DSO to the T.A. Reserve of Officers (National Defence Companies) for a period of 2 years from 1st June 1939, as an exceptional case in the public interest.

 I have the honour to be Sir
Your obedient Servant
W.G. Lindsell, Maj Gen

### Appointments – Officers – NDC

To: Sn. Comd
From: S.M. Area                                     14th November 1939

Reference A.C.I. 742/1939. The appointment of Colonel (Hon. Brigadier General) A. PAGAN, DSO, Colonel The Gloucestershire Regiment, to command the new 8th Home Defence Battalion The Gloucestershire Regiment is forwarded and recommended.

### URGENT POSTAL TELEGRAM

From Military Secretary, War Office
To GOC in C SOUTHERN COMMAND          6th December 1939

The appointment of Colonel A. Pagan, DSO, to command 8th (H.D.) Battalion The Gloucestershire Regiment is approved.

*The first two years of the war are bad for Britain, but good for him. The Nation shakes at the possibility of invasion by a ruthless foe, and her armed forces pay the price of years of neglect and underfunding. Young officers repeat the cynical maxim, 'Never be at the top when war starts,' as senior officers are swept away to appease the gods of Whitehall. The Gloucesters 2nd Battalion goes down in a blaze of*

*glory at Cassel, holding up the German panzers with their hopelessly inadequate weaponry. For four days they hold the perimeter for the evacuation of the BEF, after the collapse of the French army and the capitulation of Belgium have made its position hopeless. The 5th (TA) Battalion suffers a similar fate at Ledringhem, and only a few hundred men from either unit gets back to England. The Regiment has upheld its reputation gloriously, but at terrible cost.*

*But for him, life takes on a new meaning. He is back in uniform, and after twenty years he is again commanding a Gloucesters battalion. Home Defence is the priority, and the formation and training of the new 8th Battalion, made up of the National Defence Companies of the old 5th and 6th Battalions, is a huge job which demands all his attention. Consisting mainly of older and unfit men, it undertakes defence tasks across the county. One company is assigned to guard Queen Mary, at Badminton, and he is delighted when Her Majesty accepts and wears a back Badge.*

*As Colonel of the Regiment he takes a keen interest in the work of the Depot, and of the 30th (Young Soldiers) Battalion based there. He is always on the move in his powerful car, and very generous with offers of lifts to any men heading for Cheltenham, Gloucester or Bristol. He also becomes an honorary 'uncle' to the offspring of service families in Cheltenham. His old Sapper chum from Messines days, Ridley Pakenham-Walsh, now a major-general, has a son at the College, and in his last term there Bill plays good cricket, before enlisting in the Royal Artillery. Over a raspberry and cream tea Bill explains that he cannot please both father and the Brigadier, and has opted for something 'in between.' He is not impressed, but promises to pass on his treasured copies of Wisden when the time comes. In December 1941, the 1st Battalion, stationed in Burma since 1938, takes the full force of the Japanese invasion. One of only two regular infantry units, they form the rearguard throughout the long and painful withdrawal to India. Under the forceful command of the inspiring Charles Bagot they fight the Japanese with skill and aggression, until they arrive at Kohima six months later. The Regiment has again done well.*

'A few days after the 28th arrived in Assam, General Alexander inspected the troops. There had been a severe shortage of razor blades during the retreat, and an order was issued permitting the men to grow beards. At the inspection General Alexander commented to the RSM that he had excused the men from shaving, yet all the men of the 1st Battalion were properly shaved. 'Sir,' replied the RSM, 'the 28th prefer to shave.'

One remembers that during the long and terrible retreat to Corunna a century and a half before, the 28th were part of the rearguard. At Corunna the army marched past Sir John Moore; the men of the main column were ragged and unkempt, and they marched painfully and in any order. But not so the rearguard, who marched past in their proper companies, their ranks perfectly dressed, the men clean and fully equipped. Tradition is indeed a strange and potent thing.

*Cap of Honour* by David Scott Daniell

*The Regiment has done well on the battlefield, not so well elsewhere. The 5th (TA) Battalion, reformed after Dunkirk, is converted to a regiment of the Reconnaissance Corps. The three TA battalions have all been lost to the Regiment, a slight which he regards as personal. His Home Guard battalion is now merged with the 30th, whose title it takes. But age and the increasing difficulty of providing properly for his men take their toll on his health. In early 1942, at the age of 64, he has to face a future other than in command.*

AAG, AG 12

<u>Lt. Colonel A.W. Pagan</u>

In your absence I spoke to D.D.P.W. by telephone and asked whether employment could be found for Lt Colonel Pagan as a Commandant of an Alien Camp or P.W. Camp. D.D.P.W. said that D.P.W. knew Colonel Pagan personally and that he would have a word with D.P.W. and ring me back.

This evening D.D.P.W. spoke again on the telephone, and said that although D.P.W. would have been pleased to employ Colonel Pagan, it was much regretted that he was unable to do so at the present time, as he had no vacancies for an officer of that rank.

6-6-42 G.W. Wilson
D.A.A.G.

Forcedly Two                                    18 JUN 1942

Your tpm M.S. 13/6 Lieut. Col. A.W. PAGAN, 30 Glos. Posted hereby as Training Officer Home Guard Gloucestershire. Order to join when relieved of present command.

Sgd H.G. Vaux
Soutco.

London, S.W.1
5th April 1943

**<u>Relinquishment of Commission</u>**

Sir

I am directed to inform you that, as the Medical Board by which you were examined on 8th March 1943 pronounced you as permanently unfit for any form of military service, it is regretted that there will be no alternative but for you to relinquish your commission on account of ill-health with effect from 28 days from the date of this letter, ie 3rd May, 1943.

The rank of Colonel (honorary Brigadier-General) will be restored to you on ceasing to be employed, but you will not be permitted to wear uniform unless instructed or granted permission to do so. I am to take this opportunity of thanking you for your services in the Army, and to express regret that ill-health should necessitate the termination of your employment.

I am, Sir,
Your obedient Servant
(sgd) W. Dryland
Lieutenant-General,
Military Secretary

Major A.W. Pagan, DSO
Upton Knoll, Upton St Leonards, Glos.

*He can still fight for the regiment as Regimental Colonel. Two matters concern him, and continue to worry for the next three years. The first is the position that the two regular battalions find themselves in. Despite their proven fighting record, they are given no role that offers any likelihood of imminent combat. In May 1943 he writes to the Military Secretary expressing his concern for the 28th. 'In a letter I have just had from an officer serving with the 1st Battalion he says, 'The remaining officers belong to other regiments, and lack the regimental spirit... we have had large drafts of men of other regiments.' I do not think it is realised how much Regimental Spirit still means, and how officers and men loathe being sent to other regiments.'*

*His words are not welcomed by a War Office struggling already with infantry manpower shortages, but his sentiments are proved to be timely a few months later when the cross-posting of which he complains provides the spur to disaffection among reinforcements for the Salerno bridgehead. He keeps up the agitation, writing to the C-in-C Home Forces and the Director of Staff Duties at the War Office about the 2nd Battalion; his refrain is constant, the 61st are continually providing drafts of officers, warrant officers and*

# Chapter 8

*NCOs to other units, but are NOT fighting. He finishes an anguished letter to Major General Steele with the words, 'I hope that it will be possible to alter this state of affairs very soon, because if it continues the Regiment will be absolutely wrecked.' He keeps prodding until, months before D-Day, they are included in 21st Army Group, and given a role in the invasion of Europe.*

*The 1st Battalion, however, remains in India, on Internal Security duties.*

**Letters from Brigadier-General A W Pagan, DSO, Colonel the Gloucestershire Regiment**

**To the Adjutant General**

'The CO hardly ever gets drafts of Gloucestershire Regiment men... all these things are discouraging and detrimental to the maintenance of regimental spirit.'

**To the Vice Chief of the General Staff**

'...the battalion feels that it has been where it is for long enough, and is pining for a more active role.'

**To the C-in-C India**

'The 1st Battalion has been at Calcutta practically ever since it came out of Burma, and is gradually becoming nothing but a reinforcing unit, which is a dreadful condition for one of the regular battalions of the Regiment – particularly when so many non-regular battalions are doing the fighting. The battalion now has about 300 low category men from 46 different units, and often has to send away drafts of its A1 men. It has sent 100 NCOs home, and has had only 7 replacements... I fear that this battalion, which has a fighting record second to none in the Army, will be wrecked if it does not soon get to the war again.' Although the C-in-C replies that 'There is reason to hope that things will change before long,' they do not.

Another great concern is to obtain fair treatment for those of the regiment that the giant war machine has treated shabbily. Foremost among them is Charles Bagot, who has reverted to the rank of major, on handing over command of the 28th.

### To the Military Secretary

'Major Bagot MC commanded the 1st Battalion during the Burma campaign with gallantry, energy and skill, usually in touch with the enemy, in command of the rearguard as temporary lieutenant colonel until wounded. He returned to the battalion as soon as his wounds had been seen to... . Bagot is now 48 years old, and no vacancy for his promotion to lieutenant colonel will occur until he is well over 50. Can he be employed in a capacity in which he would eventually become a war substantive lieutenant colonel, and thus qualify for a pension of that rank?' Later he writes, 'I feel that Bagot's performance has not been fully appreciated. All the officers and men that I have seen who served with him have testified to it, and staff officers who served with him on the withdrawal have expressed the highest appreciation of his work.'

*His efforts seem to be little regarded by the Gods of Whitehall. By the end of the war he is frustrated and in poor health. Privately he vents the frustration of the regimental officer. 'Actually in the last war I had a battalion and a brigade for four and a half consecutive years, as well as short periods when I commanded it in action previously, owing to Gardiner's absence, and I reverted to company commander. Also in the last war the staff chaps like Wetherall and Needham got on – they always do!'*

*His concern for the two regular battalions arouses little response in Whitehall. As the war draws to a close, the subject of recruiting for a peacetime army occupies his mind. Once again he attempts to alert the powers that be to the importance of the Regimental connection.*

# Chapter 8

**Adjutant General**
War Office.

Often when men leave their training units they are despatched to a regiment other than their own, and their faith is shaken... . Admittedly, when the war was on it was sometimes necessary – although it was often done unnecessarily – to send men elsewhere other than to their proper regiments. We may promise the soldier the most extravagant amenities in barracks, we may increase his pay, we may bring him back to home service almost before he has begun his foreign service, but as long as we change him from regiment to regiment and then rob him of his precious sense of esprit de corps we shall never have the contentment that we must have to fill the ranks.

A W Pagan
Colonel, The Gloucestershire Regiment

*In early 1947 he writes to the Military Secretary, expressing a wish to give up the Colonelcy, 'as I am no longer sufficiently fit to do the job.' He suggests that Lieutenant General Sir Edward Wetherall should be his successor. He writes to a fellow Regimental Colonel, 'I am too ill to travel... I am sorry to be such a damned nuisance.'*

## CHELTENHAM COLLEGE MAGAZINE 1949

General Pagan was a member of the College Council 1940-1948. The Library has benefitted considerably by the large number of books it has received from General Pagan. The Pagan Bequest represents practically the whole of his personal collection of books and includes many important volumes on political and military history, many books on cricket, and valuable reference books. They all now bear a special label.

General Pagan expressed intense interest after his retirement in all that concerned the College, and for the last twenty years he has been constantly in and about College. Boys learnt to know well his car which he drove at fearsome speed across the Cotswolds. Mr Roseveare, when Headmaster, wishing to test his reliability, was driven by him to London in almost record time, and afterwards allowed him to take out any boy lucky enough to be invited. Football and cricket he loved, and attended almost every College match.

He was a great little fighting soldier, fiery and undefeatable, beloved by his Regiment and all who knew him.

*1949. The bells toll across the city, summoning to the funeral. Knots of men gather and make their way to the Cathedral. Veterans wear many medals from many different wars. The officers wear dark suits and bowler hats, but their number is dwarfed by the blazers and ties of The Regimental Association members. It is above all their day. They have come to say goodbye to 'Patsy', 'Bildad', 'The Brigadier', 'The Colonel'.*

*The cymbals clash, the trumpets ring out, the bass drum crashes, its monstrous beat echoing from the ancient walls, where the old Regimental Colours hang like dark shadows. The Regimental Slow and Quick marches have been played, the congregation as rigidly to attention as for the National Anthem. Harry Nicholls has led the cortege, his master's medals and decorations borne on a cushion. The Great and the Good of Gloucestershire process: the Lord Lieutenant, the High Sheriff, the City aldermen, they have come to join his men.*

*The Reverend Cassan, Chaplain to the Regiment, speaks: 'General Pagan was a great little man, noted for his courtesy, his courage, and for his consideration for others. For him, the regiment came first and last.' Outside, afterwards, as the Great Men go about their business, men remember in their own way.*

*'Remember at the Somme, when he got that Blighty one – did he swear!'*

*'What about Passchendaele then, comin' back in his pyjamas!'*

*'He says to me, he says, Wilkins, he says, if you go absent for sheep shearing one more time, I shall personally come to the Forest with a shot gun, and get rid of your sheep!'*

*'Remember South Africa, all that marching? We was out one day, done twenty mile, I was done, I was on my chin strap. He comes up beside me, he*

says *Give me your pack, an' he carries it for the rest of the day. An' him only a little 'un.'*

'Little in stature, but big in spirit, eh boys?'

The bowler hats discuss in low tones.

'Precious few family. Violet, of course, died back in the thirties, and that just leaves Ethilda. Can't see her marrying at her age, that means the end of the line.'

'I believe there is a cousin, Maude, down in Sussex. Also unmarried. A pretty unmarrying sort of family.'

There was talk of a very attractive mother of one of the Young Soldiers, early on in the war. Came to nothing though. I wonder who he left everything to.'

'I can answer that. He was very good to Nicholls, left him and Liliane the cottage; the main beneficiary was Ethilda, of course, but he left his collection of Wisdens to Ridley Pakenham-Walsh's boy, and one other bequest for quite a large sum to someone we had never heard of. Funny business but Patsy was a very private chap you know. Trust him to have a secret.'

The talk goes on.

'Aubers Ridge...'

'Bloemfontein...'

'The Boer...'

'The Boche...'

'The Hun...'

'The Irish...'

'The 28th...'

'The 61st...'

'Patsy...'

'Bildad...'

'Patsy...'

'Patsy...'

# Epilogue

## REFLECTIONS

Service with a good infantry battalion in France was the highest thing attainable during the years 1914 to 1918, and it is a pity that the life has generally been described by people whose outlook differed from that of the ordinary man. The feature of most books on the subject is the ever-lasting analysis of the effect on their writers' minds of the horrors of war, the phrase 'Horrors of war' signifying the periods of acute fear and extreme discomfort that war must from time to time inflict on all who take part in it. In reality 'the horrors' were forgotten as soon as they were over; time was rarely wasted in sickly introspection.

The good comradeship and enjoyment of life that existed, the courage, good will and cheerfulness of the men in the ranks, the endurance of the fighting type of company and platoon commander and the care for the troops on the part of the higher commanders and their staffs are, apart from actual events, the principal impressions left by long association with the 28th in war.

*Infantry* by A.W. Pagan

# Select Bibliography

Anon, *The Slashers*, John Jennings (Gloucester), 1965

Back Badge, *Journal of the Gloucestershire Regiment*, Soldiers of Gloucestershire Museum

Barnes AF, *The Story of the 2/5th Battalion Gloucestershire Regiment*, Crypt House, 1930

Daniel DS, *Cap of Honour*, Harrap, 1951

Digest of Services, *2nd Gloucesters, 1900-02*, Soldiers of Gloucestershire Museum

Farrar-Hockley AH, *The Somme*, Pan,1966

HMG, *The Campaign of Outrage, including Murder, Arson, etc*, National Archives, Kew

Holmes R, *Tommy*, Harper Collins, 2004

Pagan AW, *Infantry*, Gale & Polden, 1951

Pagan AW, *Papers 1929-47*, Soldiers of Gloucestershire Museum

Pagan AW, *Record of Service*, Military Secretary MOD

Palmer F, *My Year of the War*, Project Gutenberg

Record of Service, *3rd Battalion Gloucesters*, Soldiers of Gloucestershire Museum

Robertson W, *From Private to Field-Marshal*, Constable and Company, 1921

Rose GK, *The Story of the 2/4th Oxfordshire and Buckinghamshire Light Infantry*, wordpress

Sheehan W, *Fighting for Dublin*, Collins, 2007

Sparrow WS, *The Fifth Army in March 1918*, University of California, 1931

Terraine J, To Win a War, Cassell, 2008

Terraine J, *The Smoke and the Fire*, Sidgwick and Jackson, 1980

War Diaries 1915-18, *1st Gloucesters, 3 Brigade, 184 Brigade*, National Archives, Kew

Wilson, C, *Papers*, Soldiers of Gloucestershire Museum

Wyrall E, *The Gloucestershire Regiment in the War*, Methuen, 1931

# List of Illustrations

1. Boer War – Men of 2nd Gloucesters with local guide. *Soldiers of Gloucestershire Museum*
2. Sergeant Yarnall and heliograph detachment, 2nd Gloucesters. *Soldiers of Gloucestershire Museum*
3. Pagan with the winners of the inter-company shooting shield, 1907.
4. Regimental dinner, post Boer War. Centre table; far left, Wethered, who covered the advance at Paardeberg with the Maxims; second right, Pagan; far right, Foord, who 'behaved splendidly at Dewetsdorp'; top table, sixth from end, Lindsell, CO at Paardeberg, who led the 61st in the attack, despite being shot in the lungs. *Soldiers of Gloucestershire Museum*
5. The 61st team, winners of the Army Rugby Cup, 1910. Back row; Corporal, later Sergeant Major, James, scorer of the winning try, killed in France. Middle row; Pagan, 'his bald head would be popping up here, there and everywhere'; Corporal, later Sergeant, Minahan, about to be commissioned when he was killed at High Wood. Front row; Corporal, later Sergeant, Smith, who played for the Battalion in Malta and China, killed at High Wood. *Soldiers of Gloucestershire Museum*
6. Militia officers of 3rd (Special Reserve) Gloucesters, Pagan front right. *Soldiers of Gloucestershire Museum*
7. Militia. Presentation of new colours, 1913. *Soldiers of Gloucestershire Museum*
8. Pagan, Adjutant, and Lieutenant Hartman, 3rd Gloucesters, 1914. *Soldiers of Gloucestershire Museum*
9. Second Lieutenant, later Captain, Lavender, MC and Bar. 'The bravest man I knew.' *Lavender family*
10. Great War – The Gloucesters march through a French town on their way to the Front. *Soldiers of Gloucestershire Museum*
11. Lieutenant, later Captain, Baxter, MC. One of the longest surviving company commanders, he became acting CO after High Wood.
12. Captain, later Major, Bosanquet, MC, 'a quite excellent adjutant'. *Soldiers of Gloucestershire Museum*
13. Western Front 1915 – Gloucesters in the trenches. *Soldiers of Gloucestershire Museum*

# Index

# Index

# Index